YOUTH PASTOR

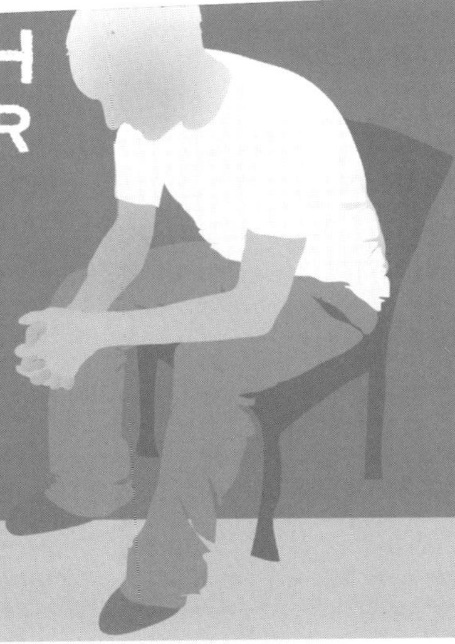

AUTHOR: ANONYMOUS

Confessions of a Youth Pastor
Copyright © 2007 by Youth Specialties

Youth Specialties products, 300 South Pierce Street, El Cajon, CA 92020 are published by Zondervan, 5300 Patterson Avenue Southeast, Grand Rapids, MI 49530.

Unless otherwise indicated, all Scripture quotations are taken from the Holy Bible: New International Version®. NIV®. Copyright © 1973, 1978, 1984 by International Bible Society. Used by permission of Zondervan.

All rights reserved. No part of this publication may be reproduced, stored in a retrieval system, or transmitted in any form or by any means-electronic, mechanical, photocopy, recording, or any other-(except for brief quotations in printed reviews) without the prior permission of the publisher.

Web site addresses listed in this book were current at the time of publication. Please contact Youth Specialties via e-mail (YS@YouthSpecialties.com) to report URLs that are no longer operational and replacement URLs if available.

Interior and cover design by SharpSeven Design

Printed in the United States

07 08 09 10 11 12 13 14 15 • 10 9 8 7 6 5 4 3 2 1

CONTENTS

4	Introduction: You Are Not Alone
6	Chapter 1—A New Role
16	Chapter 2—"Daniel Just Doesn't Think All the Way"
29	Chapter 3—Things I Never Knew about Jesus
38	Chapter 4—Flapping in the Breeze
47	Chapter 5—The Love Shack
56	Chapter 6—Holding Hands with Jesus (Not That There's Anything Wrong with That)
66	Chapter 7—Sam
77	Chapter 8—"I Haven't Felt Alive in a Long Time"
85	Chapter 9—"Am I Being Fired?"
94	Chapter 10—Sing Unto the Lord a New Song
107	Epilogue

YOU ARE NOT ALONE

Let's start there. You probably picked up this book at the National Youth Workers Convention and are now checking out the introduction to see what it's about.

So we'll start with this: *You are not alone.*

Most of the people milling around you are going through exactly what you're going through—and you're probably going through a lot right now and are hoping that this week away will give you some sort of rest and renewal. It probably will. But your problems will still be there when you get home. You might get ideas here on how to deal with those problems, but they may or may not work for you.

I'll say it again. *You are not alone.*

People like to work with little kids. Little kids give hugs and act like they're happy to see you. People like to work with adults because adults can carry on adult conversations. YOU like to work with teenagers, so there's something wrong with you to begin with.

I've been there.

That's what this book is about. I've been doing this kind of work for as long as the average convention delegate has been alive. I've been there *and* done that. I even wrote a lot of it down. I kept journals. So I went through them and pulled out some great stories about one specific church I worked in years ago, Saint ---.

I also screwed up a lot. That's partly why this book is anonymous. Who'd want their screw-up stories published for the world to read?

But I also wanted to protect certain people in this book. You'll see why when you read it. I changed names and fudged the details just a bit, but that was to protect the innocent, as the old *Dragnet* show used to say.

You are not alone, and if writing these stories down can help you get through some of the same kind of garbage I went through, then purging this stuff from my soul was a good thing.

You are not alone.

CHAPTER 1
A NEW ROLE

Abbey is my unofficial favorite kid.

We all have favorites, right? I mean, we're not supposed to. We're supposed to love all of our students equally and all that, right? But we all have them anyway. The one who bails you out when the discussion you planned is going into the toilet. You play the song or show the video, and you're sitting there with your list of discussion questions. The first one sparks a silence you can almost taste—then "the one" looks at you and bails you out. You both know she isn't interested in the discussion at all; she just likes you enough not to let you look stupid. Or he's the one who says the lasagna you made was just fine, even though you've already seen six plates of it in the garbage can.

We've all got that one kid. The one we cut some extra slack to get the permission slip and check turned in. The one we cover for when he forgets his money. The one we are truly going to miss when she graduates—the one we hope really will keep in contact after going to college. We want her wedding invitation. We want his kids' birth announcements. It's okay to have those kids. There's a special relationship there, and we get the feeling we would have been good friends if we'd met as fellow high school students.

Abbey is that kid for me. Part of it is because she came to my very first youth group meeting at the church and has kept coming back almost every Sunday for five years. And she was completely aware of her role in the big picture. She wasn't there to learn, like some of the other kids. She already had a good idea of what she believed and why. She came because she liked me, and she felt needed when I blew a discussion or blew a gasket when a couple of junior high boys decided to see what happens when you put the corn chips bag in the microwave.

Abbey's background was a lot like mine, too. Two parents. One sibling. Dad drank too much. Mom smiled too much. Sibling got way better grades.

Abbey is a poet. She can write stuff that makes you cry. I like to paint, and I would have majored in art in college if I thought I could have gotten away with it. I was on the Parent-Student-Loan plan, as I'm sure Abbey will be when she graduates. She's the kid who's too hip for the room, if you know what I mean. Other kids will whine when it's time to stop playing Shuffle Your Buns. To Abbey, that's the annoying game you play to keep the majority happy so you can get to the discussion. Nobody at home listens to Abbey's opinions, so when she gets to church, it's her chance to let it go.

She's one of those kids you let sit in your office when no one else is there. She's one of those kids who catches M&Ms® in her mouth when you toss them. When her parents caught her with a joint, she curled up in a ball on my couch and cried. As a punishment her parents grounded her from going to youth group meetings. I almost never get involved in the way parents raise their kids, so it was unusual for me to call Abbey's mom and tell her why Abbey needed to be in church. The next week she was back again—grounded from everything BUT church. She never touched pot again.

Abbey would come up with these wild theories about God and heaven and prayer, and I would just sit in wonder. I once talked about my own high school days. I was part of the geek-and-dweeb crowd, but I didn't have a lot of friends. Abbey said, "I would have been your friend in high school."

She's the one who gives me an honest opinion when I try a haircut that's much too young for me. She's the one who, on the winter retreat, very quietly said, "You might want to stay up a little past curfew or else move your sleeping bag in front of the boys' cabin door."

She's that kind of kid. She also thought I was pretty cool. Most teenagers tolerate you. A few think you're cool enough to hang around with, but they don't always invite you into their lives. Abbey let me into her life.

Her mother once told me that Abbey wrote an essay about me when a teacher assigned the "Who Is My Hero" topic. That's a biggie. That was major.

Now before I continue my story about Abbey, I need to tell you about my friend Emma.

Emma and I went to the same high school. We both played trumpet in the marching band, and we both had C lunch. Other than that, we weren't friends. Then we became good friends in college because we had no one else. Even in a group of friends, it was still Emma and I—and some other people. Emma and I studied together, commiserated with each other over our bad grades, and more than once we got stinking drunk together. Mostly it was the former and not the latter. That's important for you to know. (At some point I realized I was drinking the drinks that were made to disguise the taste of alcohol, so what was the point?)

I won't give a temperance lecture, even though I'm not much of a drinker these days. There are two occasions on which I will drink alcohol. Well, three. One is after mowing the lawn on a hot August day; there's just something about coming into the house and drinking an ice-cold beer. The second is with Mexican food. Tacos, burritos, even taco salad deserves a beer to wash it down. I'll also toast a bride and groom with a glass of champagne. That's it for my drinking.

I won't talk about the evils of alcohol to my youth group, either. I'll talk about underage drinking and drinking and driving. I'll talk about the stupidity of getting into a car when you know the driver has had too much to drink. I've given out my cell phone number and said, "Anytime. Anyplace. I'll come get you. Just don't get in the car."

Emma was going to be in town for just one day. She landed a job in her chosen profession and was now working for one of the top country radio stations in the U.S. She was trying to get one of our local stations to pick up her station's crazy morning-duo program for syndication. She called me and said, "Let's get tacos."

She was going to stay at my place, and we decided to take a cab into the city. We really weren't intending to get drunk, but we were intending to drink. We thought it would be better just to take the cab. With my apartment key hanging around my neck and tucked inside my T-shirt, we went out.

Benny's is the place for tacos. Those fast-food joints that say they have tacos don't have *tacos*. Benny's makes their own tortillas, their own salsa, and probably their own cheese for all I know. Good tacos. Emma and I started out with three apiece.

Benny's also has the bucket of beer special. Five bucks and five beers come in a tin bucket of ice. One is usually a pretty fancy-label beer, the next is mediocre, and the last three are something akin to swamp water. I remember when we ordered the second bucket. I'm pretty sure we didn't finish the third, but I don't know.

Emma and I weren't so drunk that we were holding each other up, but we were both swaying back and forth when we stood. We both got the giggles when she forgot how to sign her name on the check. We both laughed out loud when she kissed the big wooden Indian next to the door. We headed for the corner to hail a cab. I leaned against the side of a building because it felt like I needed something that large to keep me on my feet. The building let me down. I was sitting with my back against the concrete, and Emma was laughing so hard at me, she couldn't get any cab's attention. So she sat next to me and suggested we get a cardboard sign that said, WILL WORK FOR CAB. To us it was funny.

That was when Abbey saw me—sitting on the street with my back against the wall with this bizarre woman, the two of us so drunk we couldn't stand. That was when my favorite student, the one none of us are really supposed to have, saw me.

I was way too drunk to get that "instant sober thing." I'm pretty sure I said something like, "Uh oh," or something equally stupid. I don't know how long she stood there. I don't know whom she was with. I don't know where she went after that. But I do remember the look on her face. I could have criticized her poetry and then run over her cat, and she still wouldn't have looked as hurt as she did at that moment.

Emma and I got a cab and made it back to my apartment. I threw up in the bushes. Emma fell asleep on the floor by my couch. I put a pillow under her head and set a plastic wastebasket next to her for the morning. I had tomorrow to be sick, and then I had to work on Sunday. I had to look Abbey in the face again.

As it happened, that was more difficult than I thought. Abbey was at church, but she wouldn't look at me. She wouldn't even look toward the side of the church where I was sitting. I knew she wanted to talk about it, but she was too mad. She kept putting herself in front of me and then turning away to let me know how mad she was. If I had to choose which was a worse feeling—the hangover or her reaction—I'd choose to go through the hangover again any day.

She hadn't said anything to anyone about it. I also deduced she wasn't with her mother when she saw me that night; otherwise I would have been called into my senior pastor's office immediately following the service. No, this was just between Abbey and me.

I'd have given anything not to have that conversation. This was a great kid who looked up to me. More than that, this was my friend, and I let her down. I don't believe it would have been possible for me to hurt someone more. I tried playing with my feelings of guilt. *I never said it was a sin. I never said I didn't drink. I was always honest with the kids*, I kept telling myself. But that left me feeling hollow.

After the service I looked for Abbey, but she'd already left with her family. Usually they had to drag her out of my office, but that day she was all too willing to leave.

Chapter 1–A New Role

Between Sunday services and the afternoon meetings, I have several hours. I thought about ditching my planned lesson and doing something on forgiveness or being human. My brain kept saying, *How about something on being a role model, or a nice lesson on being stupid might suffice.*

Instead I led a lesson using an episode of *The Simpsons* as an illustration. The discussion went badly. The pizza arrived late. The kids played Sardines and pulled a drawer off the track in the choir room. (No matter how many times we play Sardines, somebody always opens a drawer.) It was a typical meeting.

Abbey stayed afterward. The last student finally left. (That would be Johnny, whose mom never remembers that the meeting ends at 7 p.m.—not 7:30.) I went back into the church to find Abbey cleaning up the kitchen and throwing away pizza boxes.

I said, "I need to talk to you."

She said, "You don't owe me an explanation."

I said, "I feel like I do."

"You don't." She still hadn't met my eyes.

"I'm going to have to, if you're ever going to look me in the eye again."

She put the pizza boxes in the garbage can and pounded them with her fist several times—hard.

I said, "Abbey, did I ever tell you I have a twin?" She gave me a look that said, "I don't believe you just said that."

"Look," I said, "I don't do that. I haven't done that since college. I don't know why I did it Friday night. I was with this old friend from college and—"

Abbey said, "You're always going on about us drinking responsibly."

"No." I said, "I'm always going on about you guys not drinking at all because you shouldn't drink at your age. I'm always going on about IF you drink, don't drive—which I didn't. We got a cab. I'm always going on about being responsible."

"Like you?"

"Abbey," I said. "What I did was really stupid."

"Does God punish people for getting drunk?" she asked.

"You don't think God is punishing me for getting drunk?"

"Who am I supposed to look up to now?" she said. "You're just like my dad."

And there it was. I'd like to say that I knew if I nudged her enough something like that would come out, but I was surprised when I heard it. I said "Abbey—"

She said, "Who am I supposed to look up to now?" There was a faint tremble in her voice, but she pushed it down.

"Your dad drinks because he can't handle things. Your dad drinks because he'd rather feel nothing than feel bad all the time."

"And why do you drink?"

"I DON'T drink," I said. "Not the way you're thinking, anyway. I got wasted, and it was stupid. I spent half my day yesterday with my head in the toilet. My best friend from college had to take a cab to the airport because I couldn't drive her, and I lost the respect of someone whose opinion means a great deal to me."

She looked at my face for the first time all day and said, "What would you have done if Rev. G or Mrs. H saw you?" (That would be my boss and the head of the staff/parish relations committee—and a royal pain.)

I said, "I'd probably be looking for a new job. They wouldn't have fired me outright, but they would have suggested I start looking. But if they knew you were the one who'd seen me lying in the street, they would have handed me my walking papers this morning."

She was still looking at me. Studying me. Finally I said, "I guess it was a good thing I was spotted by a friend."

She was silent. I said, "You're going to be graduating in a few months and going to school someplace far away. I'd like to think you'd stick around, but I know you're going to be out of here as fast as you can. Do you remember a long time ago when I was talking about what I was like in high school and how I didn't have a lot of friends, and you said that you would have been my friend in high school?"

She nodded.

I said, "I'd like to think that I'm going to be your friend when you're an adult, but you're going to have to see me for my faults and like me anyway."

She put the lid on the garbage can and pushed it tight; then she came over and hugged me. She held on for a while and then headed for the door. "I'll see you Wednesday?"

"I'll be here," I said. She went out the door and got into that old beater of a car of hers and drove home. I wasn't entirely sure I'd see her on Wednesday. But she showed up and brought homemade cookies, which she does sometimes.

We weren't the same after that. I mean, we were the same people separately, but she and I together weren't the same. I was no longer the teacher. I was her friend. I had problems; I had stupid attacks; I had really, really bad days. I was now a human being in her eyes, which was a new role.

You want the truth? I sort of like that better.

CHAPTER 2
"DANIEL JUST DOESN'T THINK ALL THE WAY"

I have this bizarre need to tell you about Daniel before I tell you what I did to him.

Is that strange? Maybe "what I did to him" is too strong. Maybe "what happened to Daniel" is better for the purposes here.

Daniel's family left the church over "the incident," as the administrative board is fond of calling it. They all shook their heads and said it was just an unfortunate error, and I would've been in much deeper trouble if Daniel was well liked or his parents were high givers, but neither of those things was the case.

So let me tell you about Daniel, and then I'll tell you about what happened.

Daniel isn't a bad kid. He has caused more than one Sunday school teacher to rethink her commitment to furthering the spiritual formation of God's children, but most of them concluded, "If I can just get through this year, I'll be okay." But rarely would one of our Sunday school teachers volunteer to move up to another class with Daniel.

When Daniel was in the fourth grade, Mrs. B was his teacher. Several times she had his mother come and sit on him while Mrs. B taught. When the year was over, and Rev. G offered Mrs. B the fifth-grade class, Mrs. B said she'd take any grade BUT fifth.

Daniel isn't a bad kid. I've said that twice now, but it's true. Daniel isn't a bad kid. The best description of Daniel I've ever heard is that he "doesn't think all the way." Meaning, Daniel has a thought and acts on that thought before he thinks ahead to its most logical conclusion. This is something that I myself have been accused of once or twice at Saint ---. It's something my own teachers probably would have said if they'd thought to say it that way. It sounds like something you'd read on a report card, doesn't it? "So-and-so is a fine student but does not think all the way." Daniel doesn't think all the way.

I should give you an example. (Then I can tell you what happened to him.) About two months before "the incident," the first-grade Sunday school class painted with shaving cream.

You probably already see where this is going.

The first-grade teachers mixed shaving cream with paint powder and let the kids go to town. They made beautiful pictures. (Well, not really—they painted with shaving cream.) Most people who looked at the paintings said, "Oh, what a creative way to paint." None of them said, "What a beautiful depiction of the nativity." I don't know if that was the intended subject matter, but it makes little difference because they were laughing and giggling and having a good time in Sunday school, which is half the battle.

Anyway, that afternoon we were having "snack" in the kitchen. I'd just taught what I thought was a fairly well-prepared lesson on what it must have been like for Paul to regain his sight after his conversion. (We used real fish scales.) Daniel is in the other room and happens upon several cans of shaving cream, including two or three that haven't had the little "new" tab broken off of them.

Now if you read the instructions on a can of shaving cream, it clearly states, "Warning: Contents under pressure. Do not puncture." It says that right on the label. The word WARNING is in capital letters. Yes, they also put the word WARNING on cigarette packages and people still smoke, but you'd think the phrase "contents under pressure" might encourage a more cautionary approach.

But Daniel doesn't think all the way.

Instead Daniel thinks, *What would happen if I* did *puncture the can?*

So Daniel begins rooting through the kitchen drawers, where we have every version of every kitchen gadget known to man. At this point I'm telling the other students a story about eating cookies and watching *David Letterman* when I was in college, and I'm completely oblivious to what Daniel is doing. Turns out Daniel's already headed into the next room, because he'd just found a bottle opener (the kind you use to open beer bottles—although I'm not sure this was its intended use when it arrived in the church kitchen way back when; at least I don't *think* the kitchen ladies were popping cold ones after the potluck Lenten supper).

A shaving cream can doesn't "pop" when punctured. The can itself makes very little noise at all, but the cubic yards of shaving cream *leaving* the can sound a lot like a jet engine. We all heard the sound and ran into the hall to find Daniel holding the can. Have you ever seen how much *actual* shaving cream is in a can of shaving cream? A lot. And all that shaving cream left the can in one millisecond, thanks to Daniel.

Daniel doesn't see us standing there gaping at him because his face is now covered with shaving cream. (Apparently the bottom of the can was pointed toward his face when he poked the hole with the bottle opener—all while I was telling stories about cookies and college and Letterman.) Actually, Daniel's whole body was covered with shaving cream. So was the floor. So was the wall behind him. So was the window on his left. So was the table full of Sunday school projects that were supposed to be drying until next week.

I'm going to quote Daniel here. I say that up front so I can also say I'm not making this up. Daniel (who also has shaving cream on his teeth because he was smiling when he poked the hole) spits out the shaving cream, wipes some more out of his eyes, looks at the rest of us standing there, and says—

(Here's the quote. Ready?)

"What?"

This sort of thing happened with Daniel all the time. He doesn't stop to wonder that maybe there's a good reason why the word WARNING appears on a can under pressure. He doesn't stop to think about the consequences of dialing a 900 number from the youth pastor's office phone. He doesn't stop to wonder why it's bad to take a whole pie back to his seat during the Advent potluck supper. To him it just looked really good, and there was nothing else on the table that he liked. Some say this is just being a teenager. (Okay, some say it's being a youth worker, too.) But this stuff happened to Daniel all the time.

Now I can tell you what happened to Daniel. Okay, I guess it's "what I did to Daniel."

Our youth group was at the amusement park all day. We entered the park together. I picked a meeting spot at the foot of the giant hippo statue and said, "At the hippo at 10:30." I made them repeat it back. We all understood. "At the hippo at 10:30." I let them break into pairs so they could run around on their own. "Stay in pairs. Don't go anyplace by yourself. You all have my cell number. Go." And they went.

There were about 35 kids in all—two 15-passenger vans and one minivan's worth of teenagers descending on the park all at once. We'd done it before. Occasionally we'd have a few kids arrive late to the meeting place, but we never had an "incident."

Here's my list of things I did wrong in this situation. (My senior pastor had me make this list.)

- I didn't do a head count before we left.

- I didn't make sure the other van drivers did a head count before we left.

- I didn't have my cell phone turned on once we were underway.

- I didn't check to make sure we had with us a particular individual (someone who had caused problems on prior field trips).

- I let them go off by themselves in pairs. (I didn't—and still don't—consider this a mistake. Most of these kids were over 14. The park is well supervised. I think it shows that I trust them and the whole thing builds relationships.)

Here's what Daniel did wrong:

- He left the group while we were on our way to the vans so he could buy a T-shirt.

Okay, my list is bigger.

We all met at the foot of the giant hippo at 10:30. The last to arrive showed up at 10:40. Most kids were tired and already sitting there at 10:20. We were all there—including Daniel, whose eyes were vibrating from too much soda pop by this time.

So we start walking en masse to the vans. We are one big group making our way out of the park, all together—just one happy youth group practically holding hands after a joyous day of fun. Then Daniel decides he needs a T-shirt and ducks quickly into a souvenir shop. He didn't stop to think the group might somehow move on without him. Daniel doesn't think all the way, remember?

Neither do I, apparently.

We were ALL THERE when we left the hippo. We were all there about 100 feet from the park exit. That's when Daniel skipped out. We walked to the parking lot. We found the vans easily. We loaded up. We drove away.

To my credit, I knew we'd left Daniel behind BEFORE we got back to the church. I have a rule in my group: "The car you came in is the car you leave in." No switching cars. (That makes it more difficult to make sure everyone is there when you leave, you see.)

We're cruising down the interstate toward home. (There's another story that happened on this same highway at about the same spot, which I'll discuss in chapter 4.) Suddenly, in my rearview mirror I see bright lights blinking on and off. About that same time, a cell phone belonging to one of the girls in my car starts ringing. It was a hard ring. She answered as I was pulling over.

She asked, "Do we have Daniel?"

She could have just looked around the van and seen that Daniel wasn't seated among the 14 other students. But she asked out loud, "Do we have Daniel?" We did not.

This is when panic set in.

I asked her to hand me the phone, and a very panicked mother/chaperone screams in my ear, "YOUR CELL PHONE ISN'T ON!" While I'm checking the phone in my pocket, she says, "WE DON'T HAVE DANIEL!"

I asked if they had him in the minivan. She said she just talked to them, and they don't have him, either.

I flipped on my cell phone, and it rang instantly. There were also 15 missed calls—all of them from Daniel's cell phone number. The call that was coming in right now was from my boss. I pulled off the highway.

I'm not ashamed to say that I have occasionally used profanity in front of my students. If you're on a mission trip, and you smack your thumb with a hammer, "Oh gracious!" is not necessarily the first thing that comes to mind. I saw my pastor's name on the little blue screen and said, "Oh, sh--."

By this time the other vans have pulled up behind me, and the other drivers are walking along the berm of the road as I debate whether or not to answer. I did. And Rev. G said, "Would you please call Daniel's parents and tell them why their son just called them from the security station at the park?"

I said, "I was just on my way back to get him."

"After you call them, will you call me back and tell me as well?"

I said that I would. He hung up. Again it was a hard click.

I called Daniel's phone. He answered by screaming, "YOU LEFT ME BEHIND!"

I said, "Daniel, sit tight. We are on our way."

He repeated, "YOU LEFT ME BEHIND!"

I said, "Daniel, don't panic. We're on our way."

He said it again. "YOU LEFT ME BEHIND."

I said again, "Daniel, we're on our way." I hung up the phone and turned to the other two chaperones and told them they'd have to get back to the church on their own. I traded out a few kids so the only ones left in my van were those who'd driven to the church and wouldn't have parents waiting for them when we arrived. I left a space for Daniel, pulled onto the highway, and turned around at the next exit.

While I was driving, my phone rang again. It was Daniel's home number. I didn't answer it. (MISTAKE.) A few minutes later the phone rang again. It was my senior pastor. I didn't answer it. (MISTAKE.)

Abbey was riding shotgun and asked, "Aren't you going to answer that?"

I said, "Not until I have a chance to talk to Daniel." I'd like to say that I really did want to talk to Daniel and that was really the reason I hadn't picked up the phone. But I was actually stalling because I knew my boss would be angry with me and that Daniel's parents would be *really* angry. I just wanted to get the boy and go home.

The security guard at the park entrance smirked at me. I was hoping it was because he'd seen this happen before and that a large group leaving behind a wandering member was a fairly common occurrence in his line of work. More than likely he was just smiling and thinking, "Man, you are *so* fired!" Which is exactly what I was thinking, and probably my senior pastor as well.

I found the security station, and Daniel was sitting there with his new shirt in a plastic bag. He repeated his line from our cell-phone conversation: "YOU LEFT ME BEHIND."

I said, "I'm sorry, Daniel. I thought you were with us."

He said again, "YOU LEFT ME BEHIND."

I should mention that Daniel wasn't scared. He wasn't crying. He was more shocked than anything else, but I really believe he thought the whole thing was really cool.

I asked him, "Weren't you with us when we met at the hippo?"

He said, "Yeah, but I wanted a shirt." He held up the bag.

I said, "So you were with us when we started walking out of the park, and then you left the group without telling anyone you were going to get a T-shirt?"

This was a moment when Daniel finally thought the rest of the way, and the expression on his face changed.

The older security guard who was in the office with us saw Daniel's face and started to chuckle. She said, "He did just what he should have done. He saw he was in trouble, and he went right to a guard. That's the way it's supposed to work. He did good."

I said, "Thank you," and held the door open for Daniel.

In a much quieter voice this time, Daniel said, "My dad's really mad at you."

I said, "Well, we'll get to talk with him soon, won't we?"

He said, "Did everybody come back?"

I said, "No, just my van."

He said, "Okay."

That "okay" was the last thing Daniel said to me for two years.

He didn't speak the whole way back to the church. He didn't speak while I was offering my explanation to his father (who was remarkably purple in the dim light of the church parking lot). Daniel didn't come back to church again until he was 17 and had his driver's license. And then he simply came in one day and said "hi" as though no time had passed at all.

I called Rev. G on my drive back to my apartment. I told him Daniel was with us when we met to leave the park, and he was there for most of the walk to the exit, but he'd left the group without saying anything to a chaperone or to another student. He'd been well aware of the "don't go anyplace alone" rule. But Daniel left the group anyway.

Rev. G said, "Did you do a head count before you pulled out?"

I said that I hadn't.

He asked if I'd instructed any of the other chaperones to do a head count before pulling out.

I said that I hadn't.

Rev. G said, "How about we meet in my office tomorrow morning, and you can give me a better explanation. Make me a list of what went wrong."

Rev. G was a list maker. He preached from lists. He liked his employees to list their goals, one year and five years out. He liked to have things in order. To him, I was chaos. People who live their lives with lists are incredibly annoying to those who don't—and vice versa, I suppose.

The next morning Rev. G and I had a long speakerphone conversation with Daniel's father (who sounded less purple). Daniel's father said he appreciated my apology, but Daniel would not be coming back to a youth group where his parents did not feel safe leaving him. They also withdrew their membership from the church.

Of course the whole church knew what had happened by the next Sunday. (Actually they probably knew by Monday but didn't have anyone to talk about it with until Sunday.) But they didn't talk. There was a silence about it all. Daniel's family was not a very large "giving unit," as they say. All of the Sunday school teachers who'd had Daniel in their classrooms looked at me, but none of them said anything except for Mrs. T—a sweet lady of about 106—who said she wondered why we went back for him. No one else said a word. Even my senior pastor let the incident go with a warning about being more deliberate in the list of "Safety Guidelines for Youth Events" he'd developed over a year ago.

I still sent Daniel e-mails and kept him on the mailing list, but I thought that was that.

When he sauntered into my office two years later, you could have knocked me over with a feather. He didn't mention being gone or what happened at the park, and neither did I. He still doesn't think all the way (as I will elaborate upon in chapter 5), but he's here. He's here every Sunday. He shows up every Wednesday. He drives himself. His parents have split up, as I understand.

God put this kid in my group. I wish I got to choose the kids in my group, but that doesn't happen. I have Daniel. He's going to keep coming, and I imagine he'll find a way to come even after graduation. I'm not sure even he knows why he keeps showing up. God does. God hasn't seen fit to explain it to me yet, but I'm sure that will come.

In the meantime, did you know that when you dissolve Skittles in Mountain Dew it's called a "Buzz-i-nator"?

Yeah, Daniel's back.

CHAPTER 3
THINGS I NEVER KNEW ABOUT JESUS

If you're a volunteer (i.e., not a paid youth minister), there's something you need to know: We love you. Volunteers are the most wonderful humans in the world and the very lifeblood of youth ministry.

There, let's call that a disclaimer.

For the most part I've been greatly blessed by the volunteers who've come and gone in my ministry over the years. I've had some truly super people who are genuine servants of God; and I've had others who felt it was their Christian duty to show up and keep an eye on me, making sure I didn't say anything wrong or inappropriate. Once during a meeting of volunteer leaders (meaning there were NO kids around), I spilled coffee in my lap. It wasn't hot coffee. It was only warm coffee. I wasn't even wearing new pants. The coffee was one of those yuppie expensive frappa-dappa things that, despite their extreme pomposity, I still find myself standing in line to buy now and then. Plus, it was four bucks down the drain.

Anyway, I spilled my mocha-frappa-thingy, and I said exactly what you would expect most people to say when they spill coffee in their laps. I'm not repeating it now. You've heard it. You've probably said it yourself. But if it got printed here no doubt someone would run to the Youth Specialties office and complain. Yes, I said it. It rhymes with…"Foley Spit." (Okay? Got it now?)

Apparently a couple of my volunteers found this inappropriate, and so the following Monday Rev. G asked me if I was having trouble watching my language in the youth room.

I didn't know if he knew there were no teenagers in the room at the time. I didn't know if he knew that what prompted my outburst was the fact that I spilled coffee in my lap. But I did know it was time to look for some new volunteers to see if I could replace them with the ones who had "taken their concerns" to my boss.

Gail and Stan have been with me for ages. They were there when I started at Saint ---. A wonderful couple that loves teenagers. I have a single guy named Pete who likes to go on mission trips and drive kids around. He's 30 and has a bad job at a bakery. But he's a nice guy who has a really nice collection of power tools, and he brings donuts to every volunteer meeting. I have several mothers who volunteer as well. (I try not to use parents because it usually seems they aren't there to help kids develop deeper relationships with God but to keep an eye on their own kids.) So I don't take parents on retreats, for example, unless it's absolutely necessary.

Several weeks after the "Foley Spit" incident, I thought I'd found my answer. I'm hard to find on Sunday mornings. (Well, not so much hard to find as hard to catch. I run back and forth a lot. If enough people ask you for "just one little thing," you can spend your entire morning in perpetual motion.) Saint --- has a few floors, so I'm actually trying to run through what we call "the back way" to get to my office without passing through the crowded coffee hour where I'd be stopped by at least 10 times as many people who typically need "just one little thing."

I'm on the second floor when I hear my boss, Rev. G, say in my direction, "Well, here's our youth minister." I know right away that I'm about to meet someone. Rev. G rarely calls me the "youth minister" unless he's introducing me to someone. I turn around, and Rev. G is standing there with a young guy. Tall. I guess in his mid- to late-twenties.

"This is Paul," Rev. G says. "He's looking for a place to plug in, and I think he might be good working with youth."

As I note earlier, paid youth ministers love volunteers.

I shake Paul's hand and smile at the thought of having a strapping young man as a youth volunteer. Rev. G says, "I have to run and meet some new members. I'll let the two of you talk."

With that Rev. G disappears, as is his habit.

I start talking with Paul and learn he's single. (YES! He has nothing else to do.)

I learn he's going to college. (YES! He has ambition.)

I learn he's back living at home with his folks while attending college because he just got out of the military. (YES! YES! YES! A big guy with an open schedule and military experience—the perfect youth volunteer.)

We talk for about 10 minutes. He's back in college going for a business degree. His parents don't attend church, but he had what he calls "an awakening" while in basic training. He had once volunteered for Vacation Bible School at another church, but that was the extent of his training with kids.

I make a mental note to thank God later for his many blessings.

Now while paid youth ministers love volunteers, we aren't stupid. I've learned my lesson over the years to never just put out a blanket call for volunteers because you lose all control over who comes to work with your teenagers.

Paul seemed like a great guy, but I wasn't going to let him hang out with my youth until I got to know him and ran him through all the church's appropriate background checks.

"Paul," I say, "I have about a hundred things to do right now, but do you have a day this week when we can get together for lunch so I can tell you about our program? And if you still feel brave enough, we can see how it goes?"

Paul smiles. We set up a time to meet at a burger place near the church on Monday. He goes his way, and I go back into perpetual motion.

Monday comes, and Paul is right on time (a good sign). I say, "Where's your car?"

"I walked," he replies. "My parents' place is just a couple of blocks over, and it's a nice day."

(YES! He's close by.)

We make small talk while in line, and then we take our trays to a table near a window. It was then that I notice Paul's carrying a thick green notebook. I ask, "Is that for one of your classes?"

(An innocent enough question.)

"No," he answers. "It's my book."

"Oh, you're writing a book?"

"Yes."

There was a pause that sort of hung there. It was a deep pause. You know those rides at the amusement parks that strap you in and take you up about 15 stories and then drop you? There's a pause between the lift and the drop. This was just like one of those pauses. I expected Paul would keep talking after he finishes chewing, but he keeps right on eating.

So I ask the obvious follow-up question, "What's your book about?"

(I pause here for just a moment to assure you that I am NOT making this up.)

"I'm writing the Bible backward."

At this point I not only don't know what to say, but also I don't know what kind of expression to put on my face. So I ask him to clarify a little.

"You're writing the Bible backward?"

He nods.

"As in starting with the last verse of Revelation and working your way toward the front?"

He nods again, still chewing.

"By hand?"

He nods more.

I sit there a moment and—still making sure I'd heard him correctly—I ask, "Word by word or verse by verse?"

"Verse by verse."

"So the last verse in your book is going to be, 'In the beginning…'?"

He smiles at me the way a teacher does when the student finally "gets it." And then I make a big mistake—I ask, "Why?"

He looks around to see if anyone is listening to us, and then he motions me to come closer, like he's going to tell me a secret.

(Again, a brief pause to say I am NOT making this up.)

He says, "Because Jesus was a time-traveler, and if you read the Bible in reverse, it becomes pretty obvious."

He leans back in his seat as if he has just disclosed the wisdom of the ages to me. I sit and wonder how quickly I can down my burger and get myself out the door.

We eat for a moment in silence. But I find that I can't help myself, and so I ask, "How does it become obvious that Jesus was a time traveler?"

Paul replies, "He didn't really raise himself from the dead. That was just him visiting from another time."

"But when he died on the cross, he really died?"

Paul nods. "Ummm hmmm. That's when he died, but the rest of the time he was in the future coming back to visit."

By this point I'm fascinated. "So why didn't he just travel in time to get out of the crucifixion?"

Paul shrugs. "I don't know. I'm hoping I learn that as I go along. Maybe something went wrong. Maybe he actually had to die so that we would have Christianity."

"So technically," I ask, "has Jesus been born yet?"

Paul shakes his head. "I don't think so. We haven't figured out time travel yet. Once we do that I'm guessing it won't be long until he's actually born."

I look at Paul's notebook and wonder how long he had been writing the Bible backward verse by verse. Just for some clarification I'm providing you after this paragraph with what I assume is Paul's method of Bible study. I don't know if he leaves the words of Christ intact and just writes the narration backward, or if it's truly a verse-by-verse reversal. Below is a selection from the Gospel of Matthew:

Then those who were in the boat worshiped him, saying, "Truly you are the Son of God."

And when they climbed into the boat, the wind died down. Immediately Jesus reached out his hand and caught him. "You of little faith," he said, "why did you doubt?"

But when he saw the wind, he was afraid and, beginning to sink, cried out, "Lord, save me!"

"Come," he said. Then Peter got down out of the boat, walked on the water and came toward Jesus.

"Lord, if it's you," Peter replied, "tell me to come to you on the water."

But Jesus immediately said to them: "Take courage! It is I. Don't be afraid."

When the disciples saw him walking on the lake, they were terrified. "It's a ghost," they said, and cried out in fear.

During the fourth watch of the night Jesus went out to them, walking on the lake…but the boat was already a considerable distance from land, buffeted by the waves because the wind was against it.

After he had dismissed them, he went up on a mountainside by himself to pray. When evening came, he was there alone. Immediately Jesus made the disciples get into the boat and go on ahead of him to the other side, while he dismissed the crowd.

—Matthew 14:22-33 (NIV)

What bothers me most, I think, is Paul's sincerity. He's a nice enough guy; he just has this incredibly bizarre theory about Jesus.

But when it comes right down to it, do any of us have what most people would define as a rational idea about the man?

We believe in a teacher who raised people from the dead, walked on the water, healed lepers, and did some really cool tricks at a wedding. Are we all that different from Paul?

(YES!!! We are.)

I was sitting with a total loon at a burger joint!

Paul wipes his mouth with his napkin and smiles at me. With a completely lucid look on his face and a totally rational voice, he says, "You're not going to let me work with the teenagers, are you?"

I think about it for a moment.

A creative lie would have been appropriate at the time, but I say, "Paul, I just can't."

He says, "S'okay. I understand."

He finishes his milkshake and stands up. "It's been real."

He holds out his hand, and I shake it. I watch him go out the glass door, notebook in hand, and wander down the street. He looks up and holds his arms out, peacefully, as if he's really enjoying the feel of the breeze and the sun on his face.

I think about Paul a lot. I wonder if he really lived with his parents. I wonder if he was ever really in the military. I wonder what it would be like to have your son move home with you because he was deemed "mentally ill." Then I wonder why I've been wondering to begin with. Paul certainly didn't seem like he was lying. He seemed every bit as rational as anyone else. In fact, in many ways he seemed more rational than half the people at the National Youth Workers Convention.

I never saw Paul again, but I did once have a dream in which Jesus shows up in my office. He looks just like all the Sunday school books depict him except he's wearing a helmet that lights up, and he's pressing buttons on a little hand-held gizmo. In my dream I stand up and just stare at him. He looks up at me and asks, "What?" Then he vanishes.

Okay? Now let's move on.

The next one is going to hurt a little.

CHAPTER 4
FLAPPING IN THE BREEZE

Pride is a sin.

I didn't get that from God's top-six list in Proverbs; I've been told that by Sunday school teachers and a few other learned colleagues along the way. I've never considered myself a prideful person. I take pride in what I do, make no mistake. I love my job. I love these kids. And when they do something right, I encourage them to be proud of themselves. I'm proud of them, too. I don't think it's a problem.

But I think it becomes a sin if you let pride get in the way of your relationship with God. I spent an evening many years ago with a Baptist preacher/chain smoker. One cigarette would hit the ashtray, and he'd immediately light another one. I was staring at him as he said, "You're thinking that smoking is a sin, and I'm a hypocrite, aren't you?"

I was, in fact, not thinking that. I was wondering about the amount of black tar in his lungs, how long he's been smoking constantly, and how long it's going to be before he's trying to shove the end of his cigarette into an oxygen tube. But I didn't want to explain to him that I was thinking about his dying of cancer. So I just sort of chuckled and let him respond to his own question.

He put the lighter on the table and tilted his head back. He blew the smoke upward in a steady stream while looking at me. "You ever smoke?"

I said, "Tried it once and threw up."

He chuckled. "I've had lots of people tell me this is a sin. But ya see, the seminary I went to was on land donated by a tobacco farmer. There was tobacco growing all around, and everyone on the executive board, most of the faculty, and darn near all of the students smoked. So ya can't really call it a sin in that case, can you?"

"No, I guess you can't," I said, still not telling him I was thinking about the sound made by one of those little machines people use after they've had throat surgery, and it makes them sound like transformer robot toys when they speak.

"It's not getting in the way of my relationship with my Father in heaven," he continued. "In fact, in some ways it's helped. I sound like an addict, don't I?"

I just smiled at that. He enjoyed his smoke, and I enjoyed my coffee, and neither of us commented on addictions any further.

But you and I were talking about pride weren't we? Again, I don't think it's a sin, but I've noticed over the years that whenever I start to get full of myself, something happens that takes me down a peg or two. I don't know if that's a coincidence or a gentle loving dope slap from my heavenly Father. Whenever a kid asks me a Bible question and I start quoting something Rob Bell said at the last National Youth Workers Convention, there's always one kid who says, "But what about…" and I wind up looking stupid. Not that this is anything new. I think it's because I'm not afraid to look stupid that I work well with teenagers. (Now, if I just keep saying that another 99 times, it will come true.)

So I'm driving home from the winter retreat. And it was golden. I'm saying it went really well. I don't mean it went well despite the problems we had. I mean it went *well*. Flawless. I was on fire. We didn't get lost on the way there. (That's a plus. We usually get lost.) I had 13 kids in the 15-passenger van. We had two other minivan loads and one car full of supplies. Ingredients for s'mores. Pancake mix. Lots of hot dogs. That sort of thing.

We spent the weekend talking about peer pressure. I brought along the right illustrations. I brought along all the right books. We talked. We laughed. I gave them free time, and they went sledding. Nobody got hurt. They participated. They asked questions—and good ones, not "Hey, when are we going to be done?"

That evening as I was heading them toward their cabins, Kristi said, "Can I talk to you a sec?" The others found their way, and a few chaperones made sure no one snuck out.

Kristi and I sat down; she told me how her boyfriend had been pressuring her to have sex. (Actually, I'd always figured Kristi had some prior experience in that area before I started at Saint ---.) She confided in me. I encouraged her. I told her to be strong. Have faith. Don't listen to the guy. And if he broke up with her because she wouldn't sleep with him, then he wasn't worth it anyway. We talked for about half an hour, and she finally yawned and hugged me good night, then went off to the girls' cabin.

Something similar happened with one of the guys the second night. I was affirming. I was listening. I was the supreme youth worker. When I asked for volunteers to pray before our last meal at the retreat, I got volunteers! This doesn't happen—at least not to me. So I was feeling good about myself as we headed for home.

We loaded the vans. I did a fast check of the cabins and found a girl's jacket and a guy's sock. (Both in the proper cabins where I should find those things, I might add.) I did a head count this time. And we were off. Mrs. R (who volunteers for these weekends and never seems to have a good time) even said, "That was a nice retreat." She drove toward home. I made sure the other chaperones had directions because I was going to stop about halfway there to fill the church van with gas.

We found a radio station that was in a you-are-just-so-cool groove, and if it hadn't been 38 degrees outside, I would have rolled down the window. I drove with one hand on the wheel and a cup of coffee in the other. I checked my rearview mirror and saw a few kids were about ready to nod off, and we probably wouldn't be singing last year's cantata songs again. I'm telling you, it was a perfect retreat, and I was the king of all youth workers.

This is where the dope slap comes in.

Here I am cruising along. The church van is dark blue with a big cross on the back and the name of the church on the side. We occasionally get a wave from other cars. The kids like to hold up signs and flash the peace sign at motorcyclists. We get the occasional bird in return, but then I always joke, "See? Even he thinks Jesus is number one."

Forty-five minutes from home: I'm on I-71 and doing 65. A car pulls past us, and a man is in the passenger seat laughing hysterically. I decide he's just heard something funny on the radio.

Thirty-five minutes from home: Still on 71. A few more cars have passed us with laughing passengers. I, in my ignorance and youth-worker-of-the-century glow, think maybe everybody is having a good day.

A half-hour from home: A car pulls past me, and a woman in her 50s is waving and trying to get my attention. She's pointing behind her. I check my mirrors for cops or an accident and see nothing. She's mouthing words that look like, "The birds are lumming cows oven where back brick oven." I mouthed back, "I-don't-know-what-you-are-saying." She threw her hand in the air, turned away, and sped past me.

Twenty minutes from home: I see the flashing red lights. TWENTY MINUTES. Almost there. Almost a perfect weekend. Almost. Almost. Almost. Almost. At that point my first thought was not *What did I do?* but *Thank goodness Mrs. R wasn't behind me—or worse, in the van with me!*

I pulled over and turned to look at the crew of teenagers who were all looking back at me. I said, "Say nothing. Do nothing."

I put both hands on the wheel and waited for the officer. He tapped on my window and made that rolling motion with his finger. I rolled down the window and the officer said, "Do you have any idea why I stopped you?"

I said, "No, I have no idea."

He said, "Would you step out of your vehicle, please?"

At this point I still hadn't yet connected the cars that had passed me on the highway with the reason the officer pulled me over. I got out of the van and closed the door. The officer motioned for me to come to the back of the van, where a whole lot of things suddenly started to make sense. There, hanging from the back window of the church van—bras. Lots and lots of bras. Probably 20 of them. (Mostly small white ones). There was even a blue one and a black lace number—I will not even begin to speculate who those belonged to. Not only had the girls in the van somehow removed their undergarments without me knowing, but they'd also managed to go through the luggage in the back to find more, slipped all the bras out the rear window, and then closed the window to hold them in place. The church van had become a rolling advertisement for underwear.

The cop looked as though he was trying not to laugh. He said, "You a minister?"

I said I was.

He said, "I'm a Catholic myself, but I think next week I'm coming to your church."

I just stood there in disbelief. The windows in the church van are tinted, but I could feel the eyes on me.

The officer said, "I can't give you a ticket, but I think you should find a new place to dry your wet things next time." He almost made one of those snorting sounds.

I knocked on the rear window. The window popped open and the undergarments quickly slipped into the van.

"You have a nice day now," the cop said, returning to his car. I stood by the van for a while, long after he pulled back on the road. I was embarrassed, and I was angry. What would I say if this got back to the staff relations committee? Okay forget "if." What was I going to say WHEN this got back to the administrative board?

I got in the van and pulled back on the road. It was really, really quiet.

I started thinking about my speech. I was composing the right words so I could drive around the block a few times before pulling back into the church parking lot. I was thinking of how to bring up inappropriate behavior and poor timing choices. I was, after all, supposedly Youth Minister of the Decade.

Then I heard a voice in my head that said, "Rev. H."

Rev. H was the senior pastor of my church when I was in youth group. He would sometimes come with us when we went on retreats. One year some of us took his boxers from the shower house and ran them up a flagpole.

Our youth minister—who was just a poor volunteer and didn't deserve half the things we did to her—blew up. It was probably just the last straw in a long weekend of misbehavior. Sherri was yelling at us, while she tried to unwrap the cord from the flagpole and get the senior pastor's boxers down, when Rev. H came up behind her. His hair was still wet from the shower, so we all pretty much knew he was going commando at that moment.

Sherri turned around and said, "I'm sorry, Reverend. I'll fix this in just a moment and then—"

Rev. H took two steps back, stood at attention, saluted his own drawers, and turned to go back to his cabin.

Of course, as kids we took that as a validation of our misbehavior, and it only cemented the ongoing torture of Sherri. She finished out the year and then informed the administrative board that she would no longer be running the youth program. Several parents gave her such a hard time about walking away that she finally did it permanently and found another church.

I could almost feel the tension radiating from the back of the van. Still none of them said a word. We crossed the township line and passed the fast-food joint where we met on Wednesdays before Bible study.

Finally, one of the girls said, "You're not going to say anything, are you?"

There's a question youth ministers get to deal with quite a bit.

If you say something, you risk losing the kids, losing their trust, losing what few cool points you may have built up. And if you don't say anything, then you run the risk of losing your job, or losing the parents' trust, or losing whatever authority you may have built up.

I mean, what would *you* do?

I circled the block next to the church three times. Not one word from the back. They all knew I was thinking about the "you're not going to say anything…" question.

Finally, I pulled into the church parking lot. We were about 20 minutes later than I'd said we'd be, which for us is about right on time. (It's amazing how parents will count the minutes you're late getting home from a trip—but ask them to pick up their kids at 7:30 p.m. on Sundays and see how many you're still babysitting until 8 p.m.)

There were parents waiting and smiling. I got out of the van and waved to the crowd. "Sorry we're late," I said. "We got held up on the way home."

And that was it. That was as close as I ever came to mentioning this vanload of flag-flying teenagers to their parents. I watched them closely as we unloaded the sleeping bags and duffels. I watched the guys; most would never say a word—except maybe to their friends at school. ("I know what color bra Kristi wears"—big, dumb talk like that.)

But I weighed my options and said nothing, deciding it would be one of those stories that gets retold every couple of years. I have a few of those stories, which get appropriately exaggerated. I'm sure a decade from now this story will turn into the cop pulling his gun or me breaking down in tears in front of the officer. Someone will make a joke about me waving my own undergarments around, but I'm perfectly content to wait and see.

CHAPTER 5
THE LOVE SHACK

Let me tell you about our church. (You have to get this part, or you'll have a lot of nagging questions at the end of this chapter.) We have a large church, but not one of those mega multibuilding places. The sanctuary seats about 600. We have a fellowship hall, a Sunday school wing, a huge kitchen, and administrative offices. The place was built in the '70s, at a time when architects often added a tunnel feature to the buildings they designed. So beneath our church there is a large tunnel that ends in an open room the size of a half gymnasium. There's also a side door that lets you into a room of furnaces and storage.

All the walls of this room are made of gray concrete. The lighting consists of bare bulbs hanging from the ceiling. There are two staircases—one leads to the choir room on the first floor, the other leads to the front of the sanctuary in a small room behind the organ. One of the advantages is that a groom can prepare for a wedding and then simply walk with the minister through the tunnel and come up in the sacristy. I don't know if that was the original idea. It seems like a lot of work for just a groom tunnel and some storage, but that's the result.

Every year our church has a massive three-day rummage sale. People donate tons of bakeware, clothing, books, broken appliances, and furniture; and the half-gym becomes the catchall place to put this stuff until the sale. It's not a pleasant smelling room. It sort of smells like an attic, which is strange since it's really a basement.

Over the years the youth have claimed this area. They arrange the furniture so it looks like a living room. There are even lamps and televisions. So the basement becomes a sort of unofficial revolving youth room. The youth are told to stay out of this area, but everyone mostly looks the other way. As long as the students aren't breaking things, most people couldn't care less. Still, I try to keep this door locked on Sunday nights. I've led a few worship services down there (for effect), but on the whole it's not part of the official youth program.

One summer night the youth talked me into hosting a weekend lock-in. I don't like lock-ins. I don't mind them, but I don't like them. If I go without sleep, I get cranky. If possible I try to have at least three or four chaperones on hand, so two of them can always be awake. Because no matter how hard we try, there are always kids who will stay up all night.

Daniel was back in the group by this time. He'd been gone for a few years since the amusement park incident (chapter 2), and then one day he just strolled into the church. He was now a senior. He was also about a foot taller, broader in the shoulders, AND his skin had cleared up. He'd also let his hair grow. It was now long on the sides with one piece that seemed to fall into his face, which several of our girl members thought was "adorable." This was Daniel. The kid who liked to punch holes in shaving cream cans and brought homemade silly putty to the Sunday services. This was the kid who liked to sneak up behind girls and belch in their ears.

Apparently all past behavior is instantly forgiven when you've become adorable. I discovered that my "girl attendance" went up when Daniel said he was going to be at a meeting or event. So I didn't complain. I hid the shaving cream and locked the craft closet, but I didn't complain.

Daniel was no longer interested in shaving cream. (He was using it to shave instead of decorate the walls of the fellowship hall.) Daniel informed everyone that he was going to be at the lock-in, and the girls became dreamy eyed. During one meeting he asked what they were supposed to wear to sleep in at the lock-in. I told him pretty much anything he would wear at home.

He looked at me and said, "But I sleep in the raw."

I walked right into that one. The girls all looked at each other and smiled. Daniel looked at me, fully aware that the girls were all looking at him. I said, "Daniel, I'm sure you can find something appropriate to wear—or else we could find a lady's nightgown in the rummage sale room, if you'd be more comfortable."

Daniel replied, "Yeah, I'm sure you'd like to see me in that."

When I was in college, my friend Emma used to say that people who knew they were cute were really just annoying. Daniel was certainly enjoying his newfound fame as a "hottie" and he was going to milk it for all he was worth. I chose to let the comment slide.

But the girls giggled like it was the funniest thing they'd ever heard. I was really surprised at the ones who'd fought vigorously during our debates about women clergy and women standing up for themselves—and here they were acting like a bunch of, well, giggling schoolgirls.

We set the lock-in for a Saturday. Kids could show up in the middle of the afternoon. We'd play games, make cookies, eat uncomfortable amounts of pizza, watch lots of movies, do a little worship thing around 1 a.m., and then hit the sleeping bags. Then we'd get donuts in the morning and go to the first service. We'd sit in the balcony so just in case anyone dozed off, only the choir and the pastors would know.

We did a very nice worship service in the sanctuary. The kids actually like worshiping in there when the lights are out, and we all stand around one candle that I've placed on the altar. I played some Crowder. We had communion. And that was it. Short, sweet, and very cool.

We headed for the sleeping bags. Our youth room is pretty big. It can be divided in two rooms by a movable wall that folds up like an accordion and hides in the concrete. I pulled this halfway closed and put the girls on one side and the guys on the other. There were no arguments. It was 1:30 a.m. One of my chaperones, Stan, asked me if we were going to take shifts staying awake. I said I didn't think it was necessary. Most of the group looked like they might actually sleep, and those who weren't tired would probably just whisper and giggle until four. Stan curled up on a couch on the guys' side. His wife, Gail, claimed another couch on the girls' side. And I put my air mattress between the two rooms.

About 4 a.m. I felt a hand on my shoulder. It was Gail. She said, "I think our cozy-birds are missing." *Cozy-birds.* I love the way she talks. Anyway, I got up and quietly did some checking. Sure enough, Daniel and Kristi were both AWOL.

I started the search. There are alarms on the outside doors of our building, so I was pretty sure they didn't leave the premises. I began checking Sunday school rooms, the kitchen, and the sanctuary. (Sometimes I've had kids sneak into the sanctuary and stay up all night talking.) After making the rounds on both floors, I slowly started to think there was only one place left to go. Maybe Stan had unlocked the door during Sardines. Maybe the custodian (a nice guy, but older than dirt) had accidentally left the door to the tunnel unlocked. I didn't know, but I knew that was the last place I had to search.

I walked down the steps, and sure enough the door was unlocked. The lights were out, but the window in the door let in just enough light from the outer stairs to illuminate the tunnel. I walked quietly down the hall. Why I didn't call out here, I don't know—I wish I had. I could have yelled, "You down here?" but I didn't. I guess in my mind I thought I could catch them at something. Or maybe I believed they weren't even in the tunnel.

As I came upon the rummage sale storage room, I heard the unmistakable sounds of "rustling." I heard kissing. I momentarily thought I would jump from around the corner and yell "HA!" in a loud voice and scare the heck out of them. But then I thought, *That's not what the cool youth minister would do*. No, the cool youth minister would say something funny, and then they'd have to go back to the youth room.

I peeked around the corner. There in the dim light of a single bulb were Daniel and Kristi—on the couch, completely naked, and both enjoying each other's company to the fullest extent that you can enjoy another person's company.

BUT I was the cool youth minister. So I did exactly what a cool minister should do. I went ballistic.

"WHAT DO YOU THINK YOU'RE DOING?!?!"

Yeah, that's me. The cool youth minister.

They both screamed. Kristi jumped and tried to grab her clothes. Daniel did the same, but tripped trying to get his pants on and fell down. I stepped back around the corner and waited. Kristi started to cry. She kept saying, "Please don't call my mom. Please don't call my mom." Daniel let forth with a string of cusswords.

They got dressed and came around the corner in a matter of seconds. Kristi was still saying, "Please don't call my mother."

I said, "Kristi, what do you think I'm going to do? Say, 'Oops. Sorry to interrupt—have fun'?"

I started walking and they followed. We went up the stairs, and I had them sit in the reception area while I made phone calls. Kristi was openly crying by this time, and Daniel was trying to pull his "Mr. Logic-Man" act. He was putting on his most serious face and saying, "We're really, really sorry. You don't have to call our parents. We're not going to do it again."

I told Daniel to sit down.

I called my boss first. He listened and then said, "Is this something that could wait until morning?"

I told him I didn't want the parents to think that I didn't think it was serious, and I just wanted him to know because he was probably going to be getting calls from them in about 30 minutes.

He said, "Okay. I'll talk with you tomorrow."

I hung up and called Kristi's mom. Her folks have been separated for a while now. When she answered, I said who I was and then immediately added, "Nobody is hurt."

She asked, "What's wrong?"

I said, "I found Kristi someplace where she wasn't supposed to be with someone she wasn't supposed to be with."

Kristi's mom said, "She was having sex again?"

I said, "Yes. I need you to come get her."

Kristi's mom said, "I'll be there in 20 minutes." She didn't say goodbye.

I called Daniel's home and got a very sleepy voice that said, "This had better be good."

I told Daniel's father who I was and that I needed him to come and get his son.

His father said, "What'd he do?"

I told him that I'd found Daniel and a girl having sex in the church basement.

The pause was very, very long. Finally his father said, "You can't keep him there? Shove him in a room or something, and I'll get him in the morning. If I pick him up now, I might have to beat him."

I said, "I don't think that would be a good idea, but, yes, you need to come and get Daniel. Tomorrow we'll talk on the phone and come up with a time when we can all meet together."

His father let out a long sigh. "The girl," he began, "was she…I mean, were they…I mean…all the way?"

I said, "Yes, I'm fairly certain they were."

He said, "Okay," and hung up.

I walked into the reception area and looked at the two of them. I said, "Stay here." Kristi started to cry again. Daniel looked at me angrily.

I went back upstairs and woke up Stan and Gail. I took them out into the hall and told them what was happening. Stan said, "You want me to be there with you when the parents come?"

I said that wasn't necessary. He said okay, and that was the end of our conversation. Stan went back to his couch, and Gail stood there looking at me.

I said, "Thank you for waking me."

She said I wasn't going to be very grateful later on. She half smiled and went back to her couch.

I arrived back in the reception lounge about the same time as Kristi's mom. I unlocked the door to let her in. Kristi was looking at the floor. Another minivan pulled up, and Daniel's mom—not his dad—got out. The two women looked at each other. I wasn't sure they'd ever met before. They didn't speak, but Kristi's mom's look seemed to say, "Your son is a rapist." Daniel's mom's look said, "Your daughter is a slut."

The two teens stood up and walked out the door. I told the mothers I'd call them tomorrow. They both looked at me with looks that said, "This is *your* fault" and left. I locked the door behind them. I almost went up to the room again, but I decided I wanted to have a chat with God. I sat in the balcony. The same spot where I'd been sitting a few hours ago. I looked up at the ceiling and said, "You know, there are easier ways to let me know I haven't taught a lesson about sex in a long time."

The ceiling didn't say anything back.

CHAPTER 6
HOLDING HANDS WITH JESUS, (NOT THAT THERE'S ANYTHING WRONG WITH THAT)

I'd just finished my first summer at Saint ---, and I was really green. I had a few lousy years of experience under my belt, and this was the biggest church I'd ever worked in. Actually, I had one brief stint in a megachurch, but that lasted about four months, so I don't count it.

Saint --- loves big events, and the people look forward to them. The church year is planned around four major events. The Christmas pageant, which is a full-on Broadway production, runs for two nights, and they sell tickets. About half the Christian Ed budget is devoted to the Christmas pageant, and members of the congregation actually help underwrite it. There was also a long history of who-gets-to-play-Mary-this-year politics that, thankfully, I never have to enter. Doreen once played Mary. Abbey was an angel for a few years and decided she liked being a shepherd better. Nearly all of my students have some memory of being in the Christmas pageant.

In the spring we have the rummage sale. Weeks and weeks of preparation. Three days of selling. Numerous complaints about who is and isn't allowed to "pre-shop," and just because you brought a donation doesn't mean you get to look around before it officially starts. Again, I've had very little to do with this particular event besides providing a few volunteers to help tag items.

In the fall the church holds a spaghetti supper. Outside talent is hired to perform. The youth are usually "invited" to come and do the dishes. (Granted, we get a nice donation to our mission fund, but someday it would be nice to be "invited" to the supper as guests instead of kitchen help. Again, a story for another time.) Much pasta is cooked. Secret sauces are gloated over and protected. The bottom floor of the church smells like garlic for three days.

Now it's summer and time for the annual Saint --- picnic. This is major. Families come back from the four corners of the earth. Members of the congregation invite guests from out of town. There are games and smoking barbeque equipment, a softball game, and a pie contest that is the source of much jealously and politicking.

The year before I arrived there was some sort of controversy about Mr. G entering the pie contest with his wife's recipe. Mrs. G had apparently won with that pie in the past, but since she ran off with her aerobics instructor six months before, the entry was tainted. No joke. The whispering and gossiping continued. A special meeting was called, and a subcommittee was formed regarding pie-contest rules. The senior pastor got wind of this and crashed the subcommittee meeting. He said it was okay to enter a pie with someone else's recipe providing the other person didn't enter the same pie. There was much discussion in the parking lot afterward, but generally the senior pastor's word is law, so that was that.

Enter the new youth minister. The youth were usually asked to plan games for the children at the summer picnic. Lots of water-balloon tossing. A homemade piñata. Ring toss and a duck pond for the little guys. And face painting. This was something I could handle.

I also had a student named Ian. Ian was a good kid, but I could never get him to come to a youth meeting. I just hadn't yet made a connection with him that would make him WANT to come. I knew Ian was an accomplished artist. His mother told me about several awards he'd won in school. I even saw his work one time. His mother had stopped by the church to drop something off, and when she saw me she said, "Ian's in the car, and he's got some of his artwork with him." I knew a hint when I heard it, so I went out to talk to Ian.

Ian's artwork was really good, and it gave me an idea.

During the next staff meeting, I suggested the youth group could take on the task of creating and selling the summer picnic T-shirts that year. I'm not kidding. This is a big event, and T-shirts with picnic designs have been sold for years. Some people have all 20 shirts. Last year more than 200 shirts were sold, leaving just 25 on the table at the end of the day. (Again, there was some controversy three years ago when it was suggested that Mrs. B didn't actually go the picnic but simply bought that year's T-shirt the day before.)

Anyway, I volunteered the youth group to take over the T-shirts. We would design them, order them, sell them, and make a nice little profit for our mission fund. My plan was to have Ian design the shirt, thus getting him more involved in the youth group. Smart, huh? The senior pastor said it was a good idea. Mrs. C, the woman who ran the T-shirt committee the previous year, was ready to pass the baton. So we were in. Mrs. C even volunteered to take our design to the picnic committee for approval.

I immediately tracked down Ian the following Sunday and told him about my plan. I'd seen other picnic T-shirts, and they weren't all that impressive, as far as I was concerned. Lots of picnic baskets, flowers, and some had no pictures at all—just words: "Saint --- Summer Picnic 19XX." Not a lot of creativity there.

He said, "Can I do anything I want?"

I said, "Are you going to depict Scripture verses in some sort of violent or disgusting manner that would be inappropriate for a family event?"

He said, "Not anymore." (He was kidding.)

I said, "Okay then."

The only guideline was that the artwork had to be all one color. It would probably be either black on a light-colored shirt or white on a black or navy blue shirt. I sat in the balcony and watched Ian sketch ideas on the back of his bulletin all during the service. I couldn't wait to see what he came up with.

Two weeks later, and well before the deadline, Ian came to a youth meeting. (I'll say that again so you know the intent of my original idea was successful.) IAN CAME TO A YOUTH MEETING! His first meeting in the six months I'd been at Saint ---. He handed me an envelope and told me I had to wait to look at it until everyone was gone. I asked him why, and he said he was modest. I agreed. When the last parent took home the last kid, I practically ran back to my office and carefully opened the envelope.

Here's what Ian drew.

I personally thought it was adorable. The simple but well-done line drawing featured Saint --- and Jesus going to the summer picnic. Saint --- held a balloon in his right hand. Jesus carried a picnic basket in his left hand. And their other hands were clasped together. It was completely and totally innocent. The saint and the Savior looked like two children on their way to the picnic. Like I said, I loved it; but I soon began to worry. I had given this kid carte blanche on the T-shirt idea, and he'd come up with a doozie.

I need to underline the emphasis on the innocence of the picture. There were no sexual overtones in the slightest. In fact, the first few people I showed it to didn't immediately pick up on the handholding thing. One person asked if Saint --- would look better with a whole bunch of balloons rather than just one.

I took the design to the senior pastor. I told him how I'd been able to get Ian involved in the youth group again, and he thought that was great. I then told him I had a concern about the design, so I thought I'd show it to him to see if I was just being paranoid. I handed him the envelope.

He looked at the picture and said, "Ian's really got some talent, doesn't he?"

I agreed. But I waited. In my mind I actually counted down *3...2...1...*

Right on cue, my boss asked, "Are they holding hands?"

I said they were.

He said, "Hmmmmmmmmm."

I've since learned that this was his way of saying, "It's your turn to talk." I hadn't been employed there long enough to know such things.

Finally, he said, "Do you think he'll change it if you ask him?"

I said I wasn't sure, but I was hesitant to do so because I'd told him he could do whatever he wanted. And he'd shown up to his first youth meeting ever. I didn't want to damage what I'd started to build.

He asked, "Has the picnic committee seen it?"

I said, "No."

He said, "It's up to you then."

I said I thought it looked pretty innocent, but I was sure some people might take it the wrong way.

He looked at me over the rims of his glasses (which I later learned was another habit of his), and he replied, "You think?"

I met with Mrs. C a few days later and handed her the envelope containing the T-shirt design. Mrs. C is in her late 60s and is a sweet, no-nonsense kind of woman who said what she thought straight out. If she liked you, you were golden. Up until the summer picnic of that year, *I* was golden. I have since lost my shine. It was strongly suggested that I attend the picnic committee meeting *with* her so I could talk to the members about how important it was to support Ian and the youth of our church.

This is how I thought the meeting would go. I thought they'd be apprehensive. I thought they'd say "Uhhhh…I don't know." I thought they'd hem and haw but eventually come to the conclusion that I could ask Ian to change the hands. At this point I was willing to say, "Yes, that's a good idea."

But this is what happened instead. The picnic committee decided that the youth group wasn't mature enough to handle the responsibility of providing T-shirts, and since this was my first year, it was certainly no reflection on me or on my leadership abilities. Thank you very much for your time. So long. Thanks for coming. Next item on the agenda.

I asked that we have a little more discussion on the drawing. Mrs. R (who also happened to be the one who'd formed the pie-contest subcommittee the year before) said, "Do you really think that drawing is appropriate?"

I asked her what was wrong with it, and she looked at me and said, "Isn't it obvious?" The other women at the table nodded in agreement.

I said, "It's Jesus and Saint ---, and they're going to a picnic."

She said, "They're holding hands!"

I said, "It's childlike. Look, Saint --- has a balloon."

She said, "They look gay."

And there it was. Someone said it for the first time: Two guys holding hands, childlike and innocent or not, looked too "gay" to put on a picnic T-shirt that had such a long history of tasteful artwork. I was dismissed from the room. I took the drawing and the envelope and left.

Mrs. C caught up with me in the parking lot and said, "Is your artist going to be disappointed?"

I said yes, but he'd get over it. I was more worried that this would give him a legitimate excuse to quit coming.

Mrs. C said, "We don't do change very well here."

I said I already knew that.

She patted me on the shoulder and said, "You tell that young man that I like his design better than anything those women are going to come up with."

I asked Mrs. C if she would be willing to tell him that herself.

She said, "Sure."

The next Sunday, as the group was hanging around in the youth room, I said I had an announcement. Ian was there. He was sitting on a broken recliner that didn't "un-recline." I said the youth group would NOT be doing the T-shirt fundraiser after all. The only one who looked disappointed was Ian.

Then I said I'd taken the idea to the committee, and the committee felt the design was not right for a picnic T-shirt.

Now they were interested. At this point I reached behind the couch and pulled out the drawing in its brand new frame. I showed it around and told the group that even if the committee felt it wasn't right, I certainly did, and I hung it in the youth room.

Many of the kids wanted to boycott the picnic. They felt as though they (and Ian) had been treated unfairly. I told them sometimes things change slowly and sometimes things change quickly. The Saint --- picnic had been going on for more than 20 years, and it was going to go on long after they graduated, so our participation or lack thereof wasn't going to matter a bit in the long run.

This was Abbey's first year in the youth group. She was in seventh grade and had a huge crush on Ian. She said, "Can we go ahead and make the T-shirts just for us?"

There was just a bit of silence before the rest of the group joined in with a chorus of "Yeah!" I asked Ian if he would be willing to redraw the picture and write in YOUTH GROUP instead of SUMMER PICNIC. He said he could just redo the one now hanging on the wall. But I said no. This one was going to stay right where it was.

Yes, we had the T-shirts made. Yes, the picnic committee had a fit. But my boss backed us up and told the picnic committee they had no authority over the youth group's T-shirt design. And we never got asked to help with the picnic again.

Ian graduated that year and still sends me an email now and then. He sends his artwork as well.

He was home last summer, and he wore his old youth group T-shirt to the picnic.

I wore mine, too.

(Just an endnote here: A T-shirt was eventually produced for the summer picnic that had a very tasteful looking picnic basket with a very tasteful looking balloon tied to it. On the balloon were the words SAINT --- SUMMER PICNIC, *along with the year. It was all very tasteful.)*

CHAPTER 7
SAM

I don't like generalizations. People find out I work with teens, and they roll their eyes and say something like, "Oh, God love you," or "That must be awful." I usually say, "No, it's a good job."

When parents in church "celebrate" their children turning 13 or getting a driver's license, the congregation groans. It's a generalization we have about teenagers, and I won't make them. I think most kids need to be taken on a case-by-case basis. I've dealt with a lot of different kids over the years. All types. Good kids. Bad kids. Kids I doubted would make it to their twenty-fifth birthdays without being incarcerated, and kids I was pretty sure would help run the world someday.

I was at a Christmas party once, and someone I didn't know said, "Tell me about teenagers these days." She didn't say it angrily. She said it like someone who hadn't dealt with teenagers since she was one herself.

So I said, "I'll give you two things that I've learned about this generation. One—they are the generation most willing to blame everything on someone else; and second—they are the generation that can stand up, look incredible adversity in the face, and say, 'Up yours'."

They are childish until they are called on to be adults.

That's the generalization. My two basic theories of youth ministry. Here's one more: *Sometimes the kid with the most right to be screwed up, isn't—and vice versa.*

I had a kid named Mark who came to youth group every week and complained about his parents and how badly they treated him. Press him a little, and you'd find out he's angry because he didn't get the new video game he wanted in his Easter basket. (This kid was 17.)

Then there was Sam. He had a mother who drank way too much. Sam had three fathers along the way. The first left when he was two. The second used him as a punching bag. The third spent an inordinate amount of time calling him worthless.

Sam started coming to my youth group meetings as a friend of Doreen's. Just friends. There was never anything "like that" between them. I was happy Doreen felt comfortable enough to invite someone.

On Wednesday nights we'd meet at the church and order a pizza or Chinese food (depending on who had money). Everybody tosses in five bucks. If a few people have six or seven, then it's Chinese. If not, it's the Cheapo Wednesday Night Special at Pizza World.

Sam (named after his biological dad's father) came in, sat down, and said almost nothing the first night. His family didn't go to church. He told me later that he thought it was going to be like school, and he would be years behind everybody else. That's not how we do the Wednesday night Bible study at our church. Actually "Bible study" is kind of a loose term; it was typically referred to as BS. I usually try and take something that's going on in the news, find a Scripture or two that goes along with it, and then write a bunch of discussion questions. Mostly I tell my students, "It's just my opinion" or "I don't know" aren't acceptable answers. Have an opinion and back it up. Don't tell me you hate a certain political candidate because of what you saw on a television commercial. Back it up.

That first night we talked about free speech and how a local parents group in our town was boycotting a concert by a well-known rap artist. The parents group said the rap artist's lyrics—which included many derogatory names for women and the "way to make them mind"—are inappropriate, and that the mayor and the city council should step in and cancel the concert. I dug out that verse from Matthew about things that come out of a man's mouth come from his heart. And one about dipping a cup into brackish and coming up with clean water.

Sometimes we can get going, the time flies by, and they actually want to stay later and keep talking. (Okay, that happened like three times.) Usually, after some coaxing, we wind up with a pretty good discussion.

Sam said, "If you don't like what someone says, then don't listen."

I asked him what if he was in the park, and someone stood up and started railing against minority groups or women, would he stand there and let the guy speak or would he voice an opinion? He said he'd leave and tell everyone else to leave also.

I asked if he thought we as Christians had a responsibility to protect young people from bad influences.

He said he didn't know that was a Christian thing. He thought it was a human thing. (This was my first introduction to Sam.)

Sam started coming every week, and at one point he asked me about my Bible and where I got it. I was working with an old version of *The Message* from when it was first released. I asked him if he had a Bible, and he said no. I gave him one. He gave it back and said he didn't know how to work one.

I insisted he take it, and then I showed him how to look up verses. I gave him one that had a decent concordance in the back so he could look stuff up by topic. I also told him to start with the book of Acts. It was violent and had shipwrecks and people getting bitten by snakes. He thought that was pretty cool.

It's one thing to teach a third grader about the Bible—we give them sanitized versions with bright-colored pictures. It's another thing to teach a teenager about the Bible. You can show them all the good parts first, such as Jael nailing a guy's head to the ground, or Ehud and the fat of the king's belly closing over the sword that was just shoved into his gut.

Sam started coming every Wednesday. I invited him on Sunday mornings, but he said his parents slept late, and he couldn't make it. I said invite them along, and he laughed at me.

Doreen filled me in. She said Sam's stepfather hated him and couldn't wait for him to graduate. She said his stepfather had volunteered to help Sam pack up his stuff on the night before graduation to save time. I initially thought it was Doreen the Drama Queen being overly emotional about things (see chapter 3; and yes, I know I shouldn't call her that). So I wrote off these comments, along with the ones about Doreen's science teacher hating her—more than 40 kids in one class and the teacher gave her a *D* just because he didn't like her?

I met Sam's stepfather once. Sam had actually walked to the church from the high school, but Doreen was sick that night, so he had no ride home. I told him to call one of his parents; he said he'd walk. I asked how far it was, and he said five miles. I handed him a phone. He called his stepdad, and after much loud negotiation, the stepdad said he'd be there.

The car pulled up, and I went out to meet Sam's stepdad. When he saw me coming toward the car, the window came down and billows of smoke rolled out. I introduced myself and said I appreciated him coming to get Sam.

He said, "The kid had better learn to drive fast because next time I'll just leave his a-- at the church." I chuckled but soon realized he wasn't kidding. I told him how much I appreciated Sam coming to church. Sam's stepdad said, "Yeah, as long as he doesn't bring none of that Christian sh-- home. No offense, Reverend."

I said none taken. Sam was sitting in the passenger seat. He was pressed against the door as if he were trying to get as far away from the driver as possible and still remain in the car. I was now wondering if Doreen really had been exaggerating.

One night we played a game at the Wednesday night BS. I typed out a bunch of silly questions (one or two serious) and cut them into strips. Then I put the strips into a bowl with the ends poking out and filled the bowl with M&M's®. The bowl sat in the middle of the table and you had to draw out a question and eat an M&M®.

Sam got a slip of paper that said, "Do your best impression of your mother."

Sam launched into a five-minute monologue that had us all in stitches. In his monologue, Sam's mom was drunk and smoking. She had to keep patting out the fires on the sofa, which she'd started with cigarettes. She tried to cook and used the frying pan as an ashtray. She called Sam by the wrong names (Steve or Stan or Stu). It was funny—but also pretty evident that he was laughing through his pain.

Sam got his driver's license that spring and was soon driving himself. (He drove his mother's car because she never left the house anymore.) Sam volunteered for our Vacation Bible School. His only job was to lead kids around to their next class, but he did it with all the pomp and circumstance of a chauffer walking just ahead of his employer. The kids giggled because every time class was over, he'd do a different cartoon voice when he led them to the next one. By the end of the week, Sam was a walking jungle gym. He had three to four kids hanging on him everywhere he went. His smile never quit that whole week. He probably received more love from more people in those five days than he had during most of his life.

Sam went with us on a mission trip. We worked hard in the sun for six days. He was always the first one ready to go to the worksite, and the last one to come down from the roof. He was the first to share his bagged lunch with the woman whose house we were repairing. He was the first one to offer grace at meals.

In the fall, Sam's mother went into the hospital with two broken ribs because her husband beat her up so badly. Sam brought a candle to church. It was one of those really big honkin' flower-scented ones. The priest at the hospital told him that if he wanted to come to the hospital chapel and light a candle for his mother, he was welcome to do that. He didn't. Not at the hospital, anyway. On the way home from the hospital that night, he stopped at the grocery store and bought the big honkin' candle. We lit it during the Wednesday night BS and said a prayer for his mom.

His mom refused to press charges and went back to her husband. Sam spent a lot of time at church during those weeks. He'd show up when there were no other youth in the building and volunteered to clean the youth room or fold Sunday school craft projects. By this time the director of Christian Ed had found a wonderful volunteer in Sam. (I'd filled her in on Sam's home situation, and she was more than willing to do whatever she could.)

Sam never talked about his home life. I pushed him several times to open up, but he never did. It was as though he'd created a mental suit of armor that he could put on at home and take off again when he left.

I was in my office on a Friday, when Doreen's mother called me. She was crying.

Sam was dead.

She said Doreen was home and refused to go to school that day.

On Thursday afternoon, Sam was getting off the bus near his house when some guy in a pickup ignored the flashing yellow lights and the automatic flip-out stop sign AND the other cars that were already stopped. He blew past all of these and slammed into a group of high school kids who were just getting off the bus. Two had broken legs. One had cracked ribs. Sam was knocked down and the tires of this three-ton piece of metal and glass drove over his head and killed him instantly.

Doreen's mother asked, "Will you please do the funeral?"

I asked her if she wanted me to come and talk to Doreen, but she said no—Doreen was really broken up, but she really didn't want to talk to anyone right now. I said all she had to do was say the word and I'd be there. I also told her I'd do the funeral.

It became obvious during the next few days that the funeral was going to be very large. The high school principal called and said she was going to approve the funeral as an excused absence for any student who wanted to go; she also asked if I would be willing to sign the excused-absence forms. I said I would. She called later and said that based on the number of calls she was getting, she was just going to fax me a form and let me make the copies and pass them out. There would be more than 100 teenagers at the funeral.

Mrs. G brought her granddaughter to the service. Athena (a.k.a., Teeny) was six and was one of the kids who'd spent a week of VBS riding around on Sam's back. Teachers and administrators and half the staff of a battered women's shelter, where Sam apparently had been spending his Saturdays doing lawn work for no pay, were also there. But Sam's stepdad did not attend. Apparently he had to work. After the service, Sam's mother told me what a nice job I had done. She smelled like stale beer at 11 a.m.

All of my students were there. A few had to go back to school, but most of them just hung out and helped clean up after the funeral. They didn't want to leave. Finally, we gathered in the youth room, and I told them they could tell me something about Sam that they'd learned that day. Most were not aware that he volunteered at the shelter. Many didn't know he had a 4.0 GPA. None of them knew that his middle name was Joseph.

Chapter 7—Sam

I desperately wanted to come up with the magic words—the comforting words that would make it better, but I had none. I knew they were in pain; so was I. But it wasn't a pain that would go away anytime soon.

When I was a kid, my mother told me that on the day of your funeral, God lets you choose the weather. It was just a silly little thing that grown-ups tell kids. I've used it before, and for some reason it usually appears to be true.

We're all standing in the youth room. Doreen is still crying. Abbey is patting and rubbing her back. The others are looking at their feet. I said, "Do you want to know a secret?"

They look at me.

I said, "I bet you didn't know that on the day of your funeral, God lets you do the weather."

They still look at me.

I said, "Come on." This was total risk-taking territory. I had no idea what the weather was like outside, but I thought maybe I'd get some sort of divine assistance once we got out there.

The sky was absolutely gray. Completely. From one end to the other there was nothing but thick, heavy clouds. It had rained earlier in the day, so the parking lot of the church was still wet. The kids looked at me as if to say, "This is the stupidest thing you've ever done."

Right at that moment there was a stream of sunshine. The clouds just sort of parted—the way they do in movies—and this shaft of light came through. The clouds got farther apart as we stood there. For five minutes we watched the clouds and the sunshine argue about what kind of day it was going to be. Dark or light? Cloudy or clear? Finally the sunshine won, and we all stood in the warmth of the sunshine, even though we hadn't moved at all.

Abbey started to clap. Everybody looked at her clapping and holding her hands up in the air. She yelled, "GO SAM!"

Pretty soon the rest of us were, too. We applauded the kid who had every reason to be screwed up and somehow wasn't. We applauded the kid who didn't know how to "work" a Bible. We applauded the human jungle gym. Before we left, Doreen asked me how I knew the sky was going to do that. I told her I didn't.

At the next Wednesday night BS, she asked me when it was going to stop hurting. I said it would hurt a little less each day. She said that wasn't true. I told her that it was true—it's just that at first it's so little you don't notice.

We still use the big honkin' candle Sam bought for his mom; now it's "Sam's Candle." We use it when we do worship services; we take it with us on all our mission trips, and we light it when we do evening devotions.

I don't have an ending for this story. There's really no lesson here. Just appreciate your students. We can't lump them all into categories. Each kid is a gift, and each kid needs you. God has put you in the place you're in now so that you can be with his children.

They're all good kids. Most of them deserve better than the life they got. Some *really* do. Others will be a part of your life longer than you are a part of theirs.

CHAPTER 8
"I HAVEN'T FELT ALIVE IN A LONG TIME"

It was a Monday morning. Of course it was a Monday; bad things always happen on Mondays. (Maybe it's not that all bad things happen on this day; bad things can happen on a Friday morning or a Tuesday afternoon, too. But if it's a Monday morning, you can be pretty sure you aren't going into work singing "Zippity Doo Dah.")

There's a word I'm going to use here: *empath*. It sounds hokey and like something from *Star Trek*. (Well, actually it *is* from *Star Trek*.) The "empath" was that being from that bizarre planet that could sort of "link up" with another person and feel what that person was feeling. It comes from the word "empathy," as you may have guessed. Which is not like "sympathy." Empathy is more akin to compassion or understanding.

Here's what I'm getting at. Sometimes you can just walk into a room and feel it, you know? The air is different. Ever walk into a youth room and all the kids get silent really quickly, and you just "know" they're plotting something? Have you ever spotted two kids, and you just know they're more than friends. (Yeah, I know I completely missed that one with Daniel and Kristi. Sue me.) Ever know when your spouse or friend is really, really mad at you but you don't have to ask why?

When I walked into the church office that Monday morning, the "vibe" (and I hate using that word, but it's accurate here) was so thick, you could cut it with a plastic knife. Everybody was on edge, and I don't think any of us knew why. The senior pastor, Rev. G, had reminded us all to be on time to Monday morning staff meetings, and so far most of the staff (present company excluded) had been good about it. But even I was on time this morning.

But that vibe was persistent. Our receptionist, M, was late that morning. She's usually up on all that stuff. I talked with the mission director and asked if she felt something. She said, "It feels like it's going to rain indoors, doesn't it?" I agreed.

We all gathered in the church conference room where we gather every Monday. We all had our coffees or beverages of choice, as we do every Monday. It was quieter than usual. I attributed this to the vibe in the room. Rev. G came in at 9 a.m. on the nose and sat down. Usually he leads us in prayer or asks one of us to do it. This time he went right to business.

"This is very hard for me," he said. He pulled a stack of envelopes out of his suit coat pocket. "This is a copy of my letter of resignation which I've already handed to the head of the administrative board. I want you all to have one." He set them on the table in front of him. "I have been having an affair with M [our receptionist]. I told my wife yesterday. She has already moved out of the house. I will be out by the end of this week. I don't feel that under these circumstances I can be your pastor. It's been my privilege to work with all of you, and I truly apologize for what you are about to go through because of my stupidity."

With that he stood up and went out the door. We didn't see him at the time, but he kept right on going—out the front door of the church and into his car.

We all sat there and looked at each other for a while. It seemed like a long while.

Rev. S, our associate, asked, "Did anyone else see that coming?"

The DCE said, "It's 9:10 on Monday morning. How long do you think it's going to be before the rest of the church knows?"

The phone rang at the empty receptionist's desk in the other room. We all sat and listened to it ring. We were all thinking, "That was quick."

None of us made an effort to get the phone. We all just sat there. Another associate said, "I think we should pray."

We all prayed silently. I admit I wasn't talking to God. I was thinking about Rev. G's family. I was thinking about M's husband. I was thinking about how I was going to explain this to the students. I was thinking about all these things when Rev. S said, "Amen."

Everyone looked up, and somehow I felt I wasn't the only one who had completely missed that prayer. Rev. S said, "I think this has been quite a shock, and I think it would be best if we all went about our day as if it was a Monday. I'm guessing the phone call is going to be from [the chairman of the administrative board], and I'm guessing I'll be meeting with him shortly. In the meantime, if your phone rings and someone asks, I would recommend saying something like, 'Yes, Rev. G has resigned his position, and we are all praying for him and ask that you do the same.'"

"Do you think we should tell them what he told us?" the DCE asked. "Or tell them what's in the letter?"

"I'd say the letter will become public soon enough," Rev. S said. "Let's keep it low-key and be honest, but don't share too much yet. We've only had a short time to process this ourselves." He stood up to leave, and the rest of us did the same.

I went back to my office and Chuck was sitting there. Chuck is our choir director. He and I are about the same age, and we were hired about the same time. We're not best friends or anything, but we do have a tendency to commiserate with each other.

I looked at him, he looked at me, and we both said, "Whoa," at the same time.

I sat down. And we both just sat there for a while. He finally said, "I wasn't praying. Were you?"

I said I didn't think any of us were. I said, "I was thinking about Rev. G's wife." He said he was, too. I said, "I don't see how we all could have missed this one."

Chuck said, "Because our main source for this kind of information was part of it this time."

It was a very hard week. A lot of hemming and hawing. A lot of indirect answers to direct questions. By Wednesday night EVERYONE knew. I had eight senior highers show up for the meeting. I decided we were going to do a question-and-answer thing. I figured most of their parents were stepping gingerly around the subject at home, so I would be honest and tell them exactly what I knew and answer any questions I could.

I worried a lot about Rev. S. He was suddenly thrust into a leadership position at a church that was going through the hardest time it had been through in years. AND he was going to have to preach on Sunday morning.

The phones rang on and on as each new person found out what happened. We were told not to speak to callers who identified themselves as reporters or lawyers. We were supposed to direct all official-sounding calls to the head of the administrative board.

The overwhelming feeling among the staff was to close and lock the doors, turn out the lights, and just sit quietly in the conference room until it all went away. We did none of these things.

Sunday came, and we had a packed house. Almost as many as we had on Easter, save for guests. We filled the pews with all the members who almost never came.

Rev. S gave a quiet but meaningful sermon on forgiveness being the purpose of the church. Chuck led the choir in "Softly and Tenderly" and "Amazing Grace"—two songs we tend to sing as a congregation when something bad happens.

Sunday afternoon the junior highers mostly just wanted to play games and beat each other with rolled-up newspapers. This is what they usually do, so they were pretty much over the incident.

The senior highers (only seven this time, and all of them had been at the Wednesday night session) were tired of hearing about it at home and were willing to discuss just about any subject except Rev. G's affair with

M. So we talked about "fitting in," and I used a song by Green Day to get us going. But eventually we got into a discussion about adultery, sin, hell, disappointment, and role models. My kids were hurting; they just didn't know it yet. Eventually we would be having a lot more discussions, but I was willing to let them come out on their own. They got to beat on each other with rolled-up newspapers, too, and then they all went home.

I went to lock my office and sat down to answer a few e-mails. After an hour I saw a light come on down the hall. It was Rev. G's office. I thought about ignoring it and giving the man some privacy, but then I thought I might never see him again. And then I realized I was actually pretty angry with him for turning the church upside down. So I walked down the hall and saw him putting things into a cardboard box. I knocked, and he looked up and said, "I wasn't sure if you were still here."

I told him I saw his light. He stopped putting things in the box but still didn't look up at me.

He said, "I really screwed up, didn't I?"

I nodded.

He said, "I love her. I really do. [My wife] and I have been having trouble for a couple of years now. M makes me feel alive again. I haven't felt alive in a while."

I thought for a moment that he might cry, but he inhaled deeply and kept it inside. I figured those emotions would come out at the worst time if he didn't let them out soon.

I stood there and watched him load his box. He was never a warm-and-fuzzy-stuff-on-the-desk kind of guy. (Me? I have more of that stuff on my desk than actual work-related objects.)

He asked, "Have I made your life a lot harder?"

I said he hadn't. That my job was a little more difficult this week, but my life was pretty unaffected.

He almost smiled and said, "Mine pretty much stinks right now."

I said, "I can imagine."

I asked him what he was going to do.

He said he'd have to leave the church and probably the state. That both he and M were out of their jobs, but they had some money put away. He said his brother worked at a recreation center that needed a coach. Rev. G had always been the softball coach at our church. He said it's a part-time thing. Temporary. But it's an income.

I wanted to ask him if he was going to keep being a minister. But I didn't. He seemed to read my thoughts and said, "I don't think the denomination is going to let me stay. Not in this conference anyway. I think I'm going to take a break from being a minister and see what else is out there. I'm guessing God is probably pretty angry at me right now."

I told him God doesn't stay angry. "Look at David," I said. Which was probably the wrong thing to say, but he understood what I meant.

He put his box under his arm and looked at his bookshelves. He said he'd been here so long he couldn't remember what was his and what belonged to the church. I asked him if he needed help packing and he said, "No. F--- it." He shook my hand and quickly went out the door. During the entire time, he still hadn't met my eyes. I didn't feel like finishing any more e-mails, so I locked my office and went home.

Little did I know that a year later I'd be packing my office, too.

CHAPTER 9
"AM I BEING FIRED?"

Okay, here's what I'm thinking: I've got only a little bit of room left and a lot more stories to share. I was going to save the story about how I got fired for last, but that would be very depressing. And as I look back on what I've written so far, I realize I've told you a lot of sad stories. So THIS chapter is about how I got fired, and the last one will be a fun story so we end on a happy note.

I got fired on a Monday. (See what I mean about Mondays?) After the Rev. G left, we had an interim pastor for about three months. He was a nice guy. Retired. He had been with another church north of us for 25 years, and he had been a minister for 150 years or something. He came for board meetings (but had no vote and didn't participate). He came on Sundays about an hour before services. He preached. He gave the sacraments. He left. That was about all any of us on staff saw of him. It would have been nice to be able to talk to someone on the outside about what was going on inside. Most of us were "grieving" the loss of our boss. (Granted, some less so than others.)

In the end, it was only a matter of a few months before we had a new senior minister. I'm not going to describe the whole process for fear you might narrow down the church. Suffice it to say we got a new guy pretty quickly. I wasn't asked to sit in on the search committee. I was asked to make a few notes about what I'd like to see in a new minister. I wrote down that I'd like a minister who understood the following:

- Youth ministry is loud.

- Youth ministry is messy.

- Youth ministry is expensive.

- Youth ministry takes place mostly outside of the church building.

- Really creative youth ministry requires an extended island vacation for the youth minister.

- A sense of humor is a good thing for a senior pastor to have.

That was the list I handed to the search committee. In the end, I got none of those.

The search committee looked at Rev. G and decided the best thing for the church was to go for the complete opposite.

Rev. T was about 50. He had a short, military-style haircut. He liked his coffee piping hot. He did believe in lunch hours but not in midafternoon trips to the convenience store for snacks. He liked schedules and plans and budgets and five-month goals and five-year goals. He liked files and neat desks. The only photograph he kept in his office was of his wife, and it was in a five-by-seven frame that looked as if it had been purchased at a convenience store.

Fortunately I was pretty good at most of the things on his list. Everything except for schedules and plans and budgets and five-month goals and five-year goals and files and a neat desk. Although my desk is usually kept pretty neat—if I had a lot of paper and administrative junk on my desk, I'd never have room for my Happy Meal toys. (Yeah, he didn't think it was funny, either.)

Rev. T liked to see a large group of teenagers sweating. He liked to see them form baseball teams. He liked to see them clean things. He liked to see large groups separated into smaller groups and clustered around tables learning about Jesus. During one of our first meetings, he said he'd ask his former DCE to send him a copy of a test she'd invented for the confirmation class, which was now going to be an all-year class.

I asked him what the test was for.

He said it was to make sure the kids knew what they were supposed to know.

I asked him what happens if someone doesn't pass.

He said sometimes we have to be tough, but it was okay to have the kid take the test again. But failing twice meant waiting until the next confirmation class.

I told him most of the kids I knew would probably never take the confirmation class again.

He said I needed to figure out how to make it a priority.

This was pretty much a conversation we repeated three or four times a month. Same words, different subject matter. It usually ended with me having to figure out a way to make some new church goal a priority.

At one point Rev. T suggested one way to get students involved was to give them price breaks on mission events. Students who showed up and helped out got money deducted from their fee. Those kids who didn't show up paid the full price.

I have this one student named Peter. Peter's parents are divorced. His mother makes him come to youth group; his father thinks it's a waste of time. Peter has a part-time job at a deli. He's on the softball team, AND he has a girlfriend. If I see Peter once every two months or so, I'm dancing on the tables.

I told Rev. T about Peter and said, "There's no way this kid can get to all the events and meetings and fundraisers. How do I tell him he has to pay full price for the mission trip when another kid doesn't?"

Rev. T replied that the boy needed to prioritize.

He also told me (again) that *I* needed to prioritize—I was letting job responsibilities slip through the cracks. Church newsletter articles, for one. I hadn't written one in over a year. Rev. T said the congregation likes to be kept informed of what we're doing. He also said I should really try and attend both services on Sunday and get the youth to come to one or the other. (Apparently someone from the kitchen committee had already gotten on him about the youth who skip church, hang out in the youth room, and take all of the "good cookies" from the reception table.)

This was my relationship with my new boss. Him wanting more and me telling him why I didn't think it was a good idea.

We all had a six-month review after he started. The head of the administrative board and the senior pastor sit down with each member of the staff and go over that staffer's performance during the last six months. Then they review their six-month goals with them (goals that were supposed to have been turned in six months prior). My six-month goals were usually a month late, and I figured that was my excuse for not getting them done: I didn't have my whole six months to work on them. (Yeah, I know—he didn't think it was funny, either.)

He had a file he referred to while we talked. He'd read things off a sheet of paper, which listed items that had "come to his attention."

During my first six-month review, he asked about "the child who was killed," "the child who was in the accident," and "the children who were engaged in sexual activity while under your watch." He also mentioned "the underwear incident"—I still wonder to this day how he found out about that one.

He also shared with me a list of his "areas of concern," which included some genuinely appropriate things: I didn't actively recruit new youth group members outside of the church, I didn't stay within my youth budget, and I didn't plan for adequate adult supervision on field trips and lock-ins. I was aware of all of these things. He also had a list that included things I'd never thought of. (After much soul searching, I've decided not to list those things here. That would just be self-serving.) So let's say that half of his list was legit and the other half was just plain out of line.

About two weeks after my *second* six-month review (which pretty much ended the same way as the first), I saw Rev. T in the hallway on a Monday morning. I said, "How was your weekend?"

He said, "Oh, it was pretty good. If you have a minute, I'd like to see you in my office."

I'd been called into the office a few times. Usually it was regarding a complaint about something that was said or done the Sunday night before: I left a door unlocked, someone ate the cookies that were in the kitchen for the Ladies Quilting Circle, or someone questioned a lesson I'd taught. The most recent complaint was that I said, "God mooned Moses. Look it up!" (Yeah, I know.)

He asked me to sit down, and he pulled out my file. He said there were a number of things that had concerned him during my second job review and that much was still left undone from the first review. I remember exactly what he said next: "We made you aware of our areas of concern, and it seems you didn't attempt to correct any of those problems. So I don't feel that it is necessary for you to keep working here."

I sat there. Probably 10 seconds went by, but it felt like 10 years. I asked the stupid question: "Am I being fired?"

He nodded.

I said, "You're kidding."

He said, "I'm not sure your goals are going to fit with the goals I have for this church."

I said nothing.

He said, "Here's how it works. I'd like you to resign. If you resign quietly and leave today, we'll give you two months' pay. We'll send you the checks. If you cause a problem, we'll cancel the checks, and you get nothing. Does that sound fair to you?"

It didn't sound fair. It sounded like a bribe.

I said, "So I'm just gone today. That's it?"

"Yes," he said. "We'll tell the youth group you resigned."

I sat in my office for the last time, thinking about what I was going to do. I thought about my bills and my savings and my friends and my rent and my students, and I thought about all these things at the same time.

Chuck walked by my office and said, "What's wrong? You look like you're about to barf."

I said, "I just got fired."

He said, "No way."

I nodded.

He said, "What are you going to do?"

I said, "I don't know."

He said, "You mean *fired*, as in, get out today?"

I nodded again.

He said, "Why?"

"My goals and the goals for the church are not the same," I replied.

"Bull----."

I said, "Apparently so."

Chuck told me to come back later that evening and pack up the office. He said, "Right now you need to get out of this building."

So we left. I told the new receptionist I was leaving for the day. Chuck and I went over to the convenience store, and he bought me two extra-giant drinks. We walked around to the back of the store, where he handed me one of the drinks and said, "Throw this as hard as you can against the wall."

I looked at him.

He said, "Go ahead. It'll make you feel better."

So I did. It hit the bricks with a wonderful splat. The plastic, collectable, glow-in-the-dark cup cracked loudly upon impact. The lid blew off and the soda spread nicely over the dumpster.

It didn't make me feel any better, but I'm telling you—now I remember throwing that drink with more detail than I remember anything else that happened that day. I don't remember the drive home. I don't remember how long it took me to pack. I don't remember how many times the phone rang. I don't remember what was on my desk at the time. I DO remember the sound of that drink hitting the brick wall. Chuck gave me that gift. If it weren't for that, I'd remember things differently. He gave me that moment of "centering." Sounds weird, doesn't it? Well, it worked.

Later that night I drove back to the church with my boxes and collected all my stuff. I wanted so badly to do something like erase the hard drive on my computer, but I didn't. I wanted to call my students and tell them what happened, but every time I seriously thought, *Forget the money*, I'd think about my rent. I want so badly to say that I stood up to Rev. T. I want so badly to tell you that I told him to shove his money. I want so badly to tell you I fought back, and the youth gathered around me and we took over the church by force.

None of those things happened. I took the money. I never saw most of those kids again. That's probably what hurts the most. I remember the pain of being fired by the fact that I never saw those kids. I still see one or two (which I'll tell you about later), but most of that group…I never saw them again, ever.

That hurt. That really, really hurt.

CHAPTER 10

SING UNTO THE LORD A NEW SONG

This is a story from a few years back. I'm putting this one here because I didn't want this book to end on a note that says, "Life is hard, and then you get fired."

This takes place a few years before "the end" at Saint ---. Sam was still with us, and Daniel had just started attending youth group again. It was winter retreat time.

The kids loved the winter retreat. We drove to a wonderful place about four hours away from the church. In the summer it was a camp location for our denomination. In the wintertime it was opened for church groups that wanted to get away and spend the weekend discussing the love of Jesus. Youth groups enjoyed it because the camp had some great sledding hills.

Just imagine it: You spend the afternoon trudging up and down a steep hill. You're bundled up with layers of long johns and warm socks. It's cold. You've beaned a few kids with snowballs and taken a few hits yourself. The students are playing How Many People Can We Stack on One Sled; your job is to push them to the edge of the hill because they're now stacked so high they can't move it themselves.

Then you call it a day and head inside. Thirty minutes later, you're all sitting with your stocking feet propped up near a roaring fireplace. Everyone has a coffee or a tea or a hot chocolate. (And not the real stuff, the fake powder that mixes with the canister of hot water the camp provides.)

Maybe you have vanilla wafers, or better yet—one of those cool moms sent along a container of homemade chocolate chip cookies. Kids are watching the fire, and you lead one of those great lessons on peer pressure or cults or choosing a career or something like that.

Am I painting an accurate picture? For those of you who don't live in the northern part of the country, I'm sure there's a beach version of this type of retreat. That all-is-cool, all-is-calm feeling you get when you've taken your kids out of their natural environment to a new place.

This took place the year after the "bra incident" (chapter 4). I'd inserted a new line in the permission/insurance form that read, "I agree to keep all fingers, toes, undergarments, and foreign objects inside the vehicle while traveling." To parents, this simply looked like the youth minister's attempt at humor. But to those who knew what I was really referring to, it was a mild warning.

I had more than 20 kids on this retreat, which was pretty average. There was also a seminarian named Ashley who was spending time at our church to "absorb" all aspects of ministry. Ashley had dreams of being the senior pastor at a multiplex megachurch someday, and you sort of got the feeling that she thought she was slumming it when she came along on youth events. But she was young, she had energy, and I needed someone like that. Gail and Stan came, too. In fact, they had continued to come and serve, even though they'd seen me at my worst just a few short months before this (chapter 5).

Gail and Stan drove their own van; I had the church van; Ashley followed us in her own car loaded with supplies. (At this retreat center we had to do our own cooking.) I'm not allowed to put one kid alone in a car with a chaperone. This was part of our new behavior policy—just one of the results that followed Daniel and Kristi's lock-in "encounter." In the end, that little event in the storage room resulted in 10 meetings and an inch-thick policy manual. Basically it was a complete guide on how to hamper all attempts at direct conversation with youth and a list of every possible way to make traveling and sleeping more difficult. I'm not saying these policies aren't necessary, but in our case it simply became a way to complicate the process.

We make the drive without incident and arrive at the retreat center, where a wonderful guy named Ray greets us. He and his wife run the place during the winters. Ray makes sure you have lots of coffee, and more than once he's offered to sneak me away to have a beer behind the tool shed. (I've been tempted but never took him up on it.)

This is all building up to something; just hang in there with me.

Winter retreats usually go as follows:

- Friday night: Arrive. Get settled. Introduce the topic and talk a little about it. Nothing too heavy. Have a snack, a worship service, and then everyone heads toward the sleeping cabins by 10:30 p.m.

- Saturday morning: Breakfast at 8 a.m. Then we get into the lesson. We break for lunch at noon, and from there the entire afternoon is free. Sledding. Play cards by the fire. Take a nap. Take a hike.

Whatever.

- Supper is at 5 p.m. We spend a few more hours on the lesson. Then if you want to do some night sledding until 10 p.m., that's okay. We have a nice worship thing and head for the cabins at 11 p.m.

- Sunday: Breakfast. Closing the topic. Worship. Pack up and go home.

There. That's it. This little format has served me well. It gives kids ample free time and still provides time for those late-night worship services around the fireplace. A little Crowder Band. Some Lost and Found. A Scripture from the Psalms. We are golden.

At lunch on Saturday, Ray takes me aside and says, "I've got something, if you want it." He leads me to the kitchen and shows me about 15 cases of various flavors of diet soda pop. Not the name-brand stuff; the cheap stuff you get at your local grocery store that's named after some variation on the store's name. This is the kind of stuff you buy for a buck and a half a case. Ray said, "The group before you left all of these here, and me and the missus don't drink soda pop anymore. So you can have it if you want it."

At this point I should pause to mention that some of you have already figured out where this is going. Let me just take this moment to say that you are absolutely right.

I thanked Ray and took several cases to the dining room. I was met with the cheers of everyone who was already sick of juice and powdered hot cocoa. Everyone had a soda except for Daniel, who asked, "Is that all you have? Diet?" His mini-harem thought this was quite amusing.

After lunch we hit the hills. There's nothing like a little snow down the back of your pants to remind you of who you are. We piled on sleds. We crashed. We slid. We laughed. We had a blast.

I had most of my regulars on this trip—Kristi, Abbey, Marta, Dave, Justin, Jordy, and Tailor (or Tait—and, for the record, we were calling him Tait before the guy from dcTalk started calling himself Tait). Daniel was there in all his adorableness. Girls wanted to sit by him, they laughed at all his jokes, and they constantly offered to share their sleds with him.

Abbey spent as much time as she could sitting by the fire and writing in her journal. Kristi was mostly quiet. Still embarrassed and angry about the lock-in incident, she was showing up for youth group again. I just let her slide in easily without any pressure. She showed up for most of the meetings. She listened. She answered if you spoke to her. But other than that, she was quiet.

I also had four kids from my junior high group. Generally I keep the groups separate, but our junior high winter retreat was canceled due to a flu epidemic that wiped out 18 of our group that weekend, including the extra chaperones. So I invited all the junior highers to the senior high retreat. (Yeah, that was a fun conversation.) But between a band concert and the "it" girl's birthday party of the year, I had only four who ended up coming along. Cassie, Sarah, Padi (or Patty), and Justin. Justin was Jordy's little brother. Neither brother was particularly happy about having to come along on their brother's retreat. I told them it was practice because next year they'd be in the same group.

Let me set the scene for you. It's after supper. The afternoon lesson went incredibly well. The topic of the weekend was "God's Call," and we'd been talking about predestination versus free will: *Does God have it all planned out for you or did God give you gifts and it's up to you to choose how to use them?* I guided them through a discussion of what-I-want-to-be-when-I-grow-up. We used an example from that first *Star Wars* movie. (Not the first one ever made, but *Episode One*.) *Was it fate that little Anakin grew up to be the villain with asthma, or was it just a random chain of events?*

I also threw in a clip from the last *Terminator* flick. I score some easy "cool points" if I let them see a clip from an R-rated movie. (The recent conduct code manual strictly forbids this, but I must have missed that page.)

Most of the kids are sledding down the hill in the dark. I can hear them laughing and carrying on. Ashley and Stan are out there with them. Gail is back and forth between the kitchen and the cabin. Mostly I think she needed some "alone time." (Which I highly recommend giving to your chaperones during any youth event that lasts more than one day.)

I'm sitting around the fireplace with 10 kids. Some are playing cards. Justin is trying to make a card trick work. (Jordy is on the hill preferring to be anywhere his brother is not.) I've got Abbey, Tait, Marta, Dave, my junior high girls, a big kid named Randy, Kyle, and Zoë.

Most of us are doing the toe-warming thing by the fire. Cassie and Sarah have become good friends on this trip. Mostly out of necessity because the rest of their friends didn't come. They're sitting near me. Abbey has tried a few times to get the girls to play cards or one of the board games, but they're content to just sit near the fire. Cassie is a singer and has a good voice. I asked her if she'd sing something at the evening worship service, but she said no.

Each of us—every single one in the room—is holding a can of warm, diet soda pop. There wasn't room in the refrigerator for all the sodas Ray gave us, and I officially nixed the idea of keeping them outside. We set the cases near the door, where the cold air was coming in anyway.

Justin was first. Junior high boys (perhaps this is a "male" thing) do not suffer self-produced bodily noises as embarrassment. Most high school guys will accept a belch as a greeting, but junior high boys will actually call attention to themselves before blasting off. Justin tilted his head back, slunk down in his chair, and opened his mouth to make way for a loud, but somewhat short, belch.

The girls all said, "Ewwwwwww!" in unison.

I looked at him. He said, "'Scuse me." But his smile told me he wasn't really asking for anyone's pardon.

It might have ended there. It should have ended there. One good belch and everyone would have laughed it off. Except for little Cassie sitting next to me. In all of her sixth-grade voice she said, "That was really gross."

But when she said the word *gross*, a rather large belch caught her by surprise in mid-word, and she actually said "grooooooooOOOOOOW-WWss."

It was loud, and it was long, and no one was more surprised than she was. Everyone stopped and turned to look at her. Her eyes opened wide, and she slapped her hand over her mouth as she turned about eight shades of red in five seconds.

Justin said, "Holy cr--!"

Sarah said, "Cassie!"

Randy said, "Wow! Did you get any on you?"

Kyle said, "I can beat that," and immediately took a long pull of his soda (orange, I think it was) and let forth with something that came from his toes.

This is decision time for a youth minister. Someone with years of experience and training probably would know enough to stop this game in its tracks and chuckle warmly in a kids-will-be-kids kind of way. Instead, I chose to say, "And your last name is?"

This is a line I learned when I was in fourth grade, and I've used it on many occasions since then.

Dave opened his mouth and forced a small "blat," but it wasn't worth rating.

Zoë, a cute kid whose mother would have been simply mortified if she'd been there, stood up and opened her arms like an opera singer and said the word *wow* while belching. It was quite impressive for such a small kid.

Kyle, Dave, and Justin suddenly made a mad dash for the remaining stack of diet carbonation. Again this should have been my opportunity to put an end to this brief detour away from a weekend with Jesus. Instead I called out, "Bring me a root beer!"

Soon everyone had a fresh can and was guzzling quickly. (Ah, children. They don't understand that speed means nothing. It's the amount of air you swallow with the soda that makes the belch.)

Dave, who was attempting to atone for his previous lame attempt, opened his mouth and said, "A…B…C…D…" and then trailed off. He probably could have gone further, but he opted for quality and not quantity, for which I give him kudos.

Youth ministers who've been at this game for a while understand that eventually you arrive at a certain age when, if you attempted something over the top, you were likely to hurt yourself. I actually won a belching contest in college many years ago, but I can't even come close to that level now. So I make up for it with disgusting comments. I belched a medium-length and medium-volume air biscuit with great depth, and then I smacked my lips and said, "Wait a minute. I don't even like carrots."

Cassie scooted her chair away from me.

Sarah, let go with something that sounded like "Ooooooooooweeet."

Cassie, who was still nearby, said, "Oh, that smells," and scooted away from Sarah, too.

Kyle attempted an alphabet but barely made it past *A*.

Zoë (the opera singer) stood up and belched, "Jesus loves me this I…"—and the word *know* came out in her normal voice; everyone applauded.

Again, this was yet another opportunity for the youth minister to say, "Okay now, that's enough."

Instead I stood up and patted her back, and she put a little "blet" punctuation on her song.

Marta, who had been watching all of this with horror, said, "You people are disgusting."

I should mention a particular kind of belch here that may offend some of you more delicate readers. There's a thing called a blow-burp. This is where you burp with your lips tightly closed—in essence catching the burp—and then blowing it at someone. (It's something my sister and I perfected as children while sitting around the Thanksgiving table.)

Dave blew one in Marta's direction, and she covered her face and moved to the other side of the room.

Justin actually raised his hand, as if calling attention to himself, and then brought forth something that sounded like an exorcism. It wasn't that loud, but it was really, really long. His whole head was vibrating by the end.

Zoë made another attempt at the alphabet, and made it to *G* this time. The guys made several tiny blips and bleets, but nothing substantial. I thought things were finally winding down when Abbey made a noise that sounded like it came from a 500-pound gorilla.

Dave made another attempt at the alphabet and got only wind.

Zoë stood again. (Zoë is about four-foot-eight and has a waistline of about 12 inches around.) She threw her head back and sang very quickly, "The Lord is my shepherd I shall not waaaaaaaaaaaaaaaaant!"

That's when we heard someone say, "Zoë!"

Gail had come back into the hall from the kitchen. I don't know how long she'd been there, but she got to hear Zoë's crowning glory.

Zoë's eyes got really wide and she sat down. We were all very quiet now. (We were trying not to laugh and failing miserably.) Gail looked at me and said, "You're as bad as these kids!" She was trying to be angry, but I could see laughter in her eyes. She was trying as hard as we were not to laugh.

I said, "That's the nicest thing you ever said to me."

Justin burped with his mouth closed and his hand over his face, but we still heard it.

Gail turned and looked at Zoë, who was still wide-eyed and afraid she was going to get yelled at. Gail said, "You've got one more in you, don't you?"

Zoë nodded.

Gail said, "Well, let's have it; that will be the LAST ONE FOR THE EVENING." She said this last part with great emphasis and with all the training of someone who'd taught Sunday school for more than a quarter of a century.

Zoë stood up and opened her mouth. That was when a long, high-pitched note emerged from the other end.

Gail gasped. The rest of us fell on the floor. We laughed so hard that tears were pouring freely from our eyes. Zoë just stood there looking at Gail. Gail finally had to turn and leave, but she couldn't hold it back any longer and started laughing with the rest of us.

You might think poorly of me for saying this, but I think that in that moment we experienced the kingdom of God.

The kingdom of God isn't necessarily angels with harps and wings floating on fluffy clouds. The kingdom of God is when we're all laughing and enjoying the moment as children of God. We were all there, junior high and senior high, males and females, old and young, and we were all laughing without caring what others thought.

The others only got to hear about it later. They wanted to start a new round with fresh cans of soda; but the moment was gone, and I put the kibosh on that myself.

I don't think any of the students who were in that room could tell you what we studied that weekend, but every single one of them could recall that five-minute stretch of time and start laughing all over again.

Did the weekend winter retreat make them into disciples? Hardly. Did it make them friends? Did it bring them together in the presence of Christ? Yeah, I'd say so.

Jesus said, "Wherever two or more of you are gathered…," and I'm sure he was there.

No, I did NOT hear my Savior belch.

But I'm pretty sure I heard him laughing.

EPILOGUE

See? Wasn't that a better way to end this book?

This is just a little add-on to let you know what's happened in the last few years.

I was out of work for six months. I spent my entire savings. I borrowed money from my parents. I took a job at a music store as "seasonal help," and they were so pleased they offered me a full-time job, which I took. I stayed for four months after that.

I spent my days off looking for work. I got a lot of, "We may be looking next year."

One day my phone rang, and it was the minister who got me through college. I'd called him once a month to ask if he'd heard of any openings. When I said, "Hello," he said, "Are you still looking for work?"

I said I was, and he said, "I've got a guy in my office who needs a youth person. Part-time. You want to talk to him?"

I did. We set up an interview. I was offered the job, and I jumped at it. I worked there and at the music store (part-time), and a year later the church offered me a full-time position.

Things are much better. I love my new church. I love getting to know this new denomination. I love working with teenagers.

I've come to the conclusion that God really needs me here and that I wouldn't have left Saint --- on my own. There are kids here who are going through some serious stuff, and I've been able to help them.

One Sunday, the mother of one of my students came to me and gave me a gift card from Starbucks. I looked at it, and the card said it was worth $100. I told her it was too generous. She said this, "Before you started here, my daughter and I never talked. She hung out with kids who scare me. Now she actually WANTS to go to church. She hangs out with kids I like, and last week we had a long conversation about God. The least I can do is buy you those coffee drinks that you like, but I know you don't ever buy for yourself."

I am exactly where God wants me to be. I know I was meant to be here in this place and at this time. (Plus I met a really cool someone while working at the music store, and we are now dating.)

Now then…

Doreen is fine. I've seen her once since I was fired, and she hugged me and showed me a "trick" she can do with her eye. Apparently she can now make both eyes look to opposite sides.

Daniel graduated and is serving in the military. Pray for him.

Kristi graduated and went to college. She is majoring in education. I haven't seen her, but Abbey gets regular e-mails from her and keeps me up to date.

Chuck got fired four weeks after I did. While I kept my mouth shut and took the money, he apparently decided to make my firing public knowledge, and Rev. T fired Chuck for it. Chuck is now working in a church in Florida. We still talk by e-mail.

I received one Christmas card from Rev. G. There was a picture of him and his new wife, M, the former church receptionist, along with their new baby boy. He looked happy.

Saint --- finally got rid of Rev. T. Apparently he began a process of systematically firing one member of the staff every six months until he almost had a whole new team. Eventually the board had had enough and let him go. I don't know where he is now, and to be honest with you (in the spirit of Christian love) I don't give a you-know-what.

Abbey is about to graduate from college with a degree in art. She discovered a passion for stained-glass work and wants to design windows for churches. I have one of her smaller pieces hanging in my window right now, and it's making my keyboard look purple.

Ian is doing freelance work for a Sunday school curriculum. I saw some of his work when the DCE at my current church remarked how much the drawings of Paul in the VBS program looked like me. (That was probably the greatest honor I've ever had.)

I don't know if these stories have meant anything to you or not. I discovered long ago that just knowing I wasn't alone in what I was going through helped.

I've also learned that I didn't know what kind of good I was doing in kids' lives until long after I knew them. If you look at your group now and think, *What am I doing here?* you may not get an answer. But someday, one of those kids is going to call you out of the blue and say, "Remember when you…?" and then they're going to say, "Thanks."

You plant seeds. The problem in this line of work is that we very seldom get to see what grows. That's why God gave us each other. There are other youth workers around you. Once a month, invite a youth worker (from another church or another denomination) to lunch. No strings. No planning. Just get together and support each other. Pray for each other.

I believe there are hammocks in heaven. Stretched between two trees overlooking the Milky Way. When we die, we get to bypass the line. Seraphim and cherubim float up and down the line at the pearly gates and say, "Youth minister?" If you say yes, they take you out of the line and give you a hammock. They bring you large coffee beverages. They let you paint the sunrise.

Eventually Jesus comes by. He doesn't say anything right away. He just wraps his big carpenter arms around you and hugs you close.

He whispers in your ear, "Thank you."

And then shows you a universe of places to hide and says, "Wanna play Sardines?"